A Leg Up

A Leg Up

✦

How I Learned to Horseback Ride Starting at Age 40

Katherine Maxwell

iUniverse, Inc.

New York Lincoln Shanghai

A Leg Up
How I Learned to Horseback Ride Starting at Age 40

Copyright © 2006 by Katherine Maxwell

iUniverse books may be ordered through booksellers or by contacting:

iUniverse
2021 Pine Lake Road, Suite 100
Lincoln, NE 68512
www.iuniverse.com
1-800-Authors (1-800-288-4677)

ISBN-13: 978-0-595-38007-7 (pbk)
ISBN-13: 978-0-595-82378-9 (ebk)
ISBN-10: 0-595-38007-7 (pbk)
ISBN-10: 0-595-82378-5 (ebk)

Printed in the United States of America

Contents

Acknowledgements

Very special thanks to…

Heather Daylight, for her extraordinary horsemanship and teaching abilities and for making me a better rider; without her loyalty, there would have been nothing to write about.
Bob Hitchman, for his perspective and focus that helped crystallize everything, and for being a talented photographer.
Jim Bishop, for his invaluable suggestions and encouragement.
Cathy Moreno, for her insightful viewpoint and positive feedback.
Dan Cooper, for his amazing ability to show me how to better express myself.
JoAnne Ewing, for telling me to keep writing and spurring me on.
Sheri Anderson, for her sticky notes with suggestions that were very helpful.
Vera Reeves, for setting a good example and showing me what is possible.
Steve Nicklanovich, for his forthright comments that sent me forward.
Annie Heggen, for her sharp eye that caught many obscure mistakes.
Susan Gleason, for her keen insight into what was needed.
Linda Zanko, for her meticulous editing and technical scrutiny.
Cate Rice, Eileen Joyce, Linda Norton, Diana Dougherty, for their support and friendship.
Lloyd Westbrook, for his merciful suggestions and keen observations.
Jeannette Derammelaere, for her generous words of encouragement.

Story 1
I Make My List

✦

(October 1981)

An image of Isabella that is reminiscent of the Black Stallion

Right after my 40th birthday in January of 1981, I made a list of all those things I yet wanted to do in my lifetime. As the list was fairly long, I was certain that it would keep me busy for some time to come. The first item on this list was: Learn to horseback ride.

I thought, at that time, that learning to ride a horse would be a brief and routine sort of effort. I estimated that probably seven lessons would do it.

My plan was to take the seven or so lessons, and then, having become a competent rider, I would go on to the second item on my list.

I am not certain where this first item on the list came from. We all have fantasies from childhood imaginings—from seeing someone do something that we would like to do. We probably all have the makings of a list of desires we put on hold, of daydreams of things we want to do at some future time in our lives. As for me, there were a number of experiences in my childhood that must have gone into my wanting to learn to horseback ride and putting it on my list.

During my elementary school years, my family lived in San Francisco. The adventures I had in the great outdoors were hiking through The Presidio, an historic military reservation with acres of wooded tract. I often came home with a bad case of poison oak after one of these walks in the woods. In the late summer of 1950, two of my younger brothers and I went to spend a year with my grandparents on my mother's side. During that school year, I attended the fifth grade in the small city in Utah where they lived. Soon after we arrived, my grandfather, Daddy Jim, bought the entire series of the Walter Farley books on *The Black Stallion*. Every evening just before bedtime, my grandfather would read to us from one of these books of the Black Stallion's adventures. It was the highlight of my days when I was nine years old. I could picture myself as the companion of the Black Stallion, befriending him and then riding him bareback along that island beach, though I had never been near any horses.

When we returned home that following summer of 1951, I was given a small radio. Every Sunday afternoon I listened to the adventures of *The Lone Ranger*. Vivid images were added to my daydreams and imagination, of the mighty horse, Silver, with me calling "Hi ho" as we rode off into the distance. In my mind's eye, I could envision that beautiful, well-mannered white horse who would come when I whistled, would carry his rider smoothly at a gallop, and would be loyal and devoted to his kind companion. These childhood memories must have sown the seeds for this first item on my list.

One Saturday afternoon during my junior year in high school, I joined a group of my friends for an outing to Golden Gate Park in San Francisco. We rented trail horses at Golden Gate Stables. Once we were boosted up on our assigned mounts, we headed off through the park on the bridle paths. At the first fork, all of the horses but mine followed in line on the path to the right. Instead, my horse made an abrupt jog to the left, a shorter route back to the stables. I lost my balance and landed in the dirt. Looking back at me from their saddled perches, my comrades showered me with jokes and ribbings as they continued on without me. My embarrassment and discomfort were intensified by a brief look of mild disgust from my boyfriend, who rode on with the pack of horses and riders. The horse I had been on headed back to the barn and arrived well ahead of me. I certainly wasn't fitting into the role that I had envisioned for myself with the Black Stallion or Silver. This adventure did not contribute to those great romantic horseback-riding scenes. Though it may have dimmed the glow a bit, somehow that disillusionment did not erase or obliterate those early fantasies.

Many years later in October of 1977, I went hiking with my husband along the Tennessee Valley Trail in southern Marin County. I looked across the narrow valley and saw a horse and rider racing along the base of the ridge. As I watched, the horse splashed into a large puddle of water on the trail. The rider let out a loud, joyous shout of surprise and exhilaration as the water and mud sprayed up from below. That musical sound echoed down the valley and continued echoing in my head for years after. The scene of that horse and rider was a vision of great enjoyment and harmonious companionship. Those early childhood visions were rekindled. I wanted this great rush for myself. I wanted to have whatever feeling made that rider yell out with such joy. I longed to be able to ride like that, to truly live the daydreams of my youth. I did not want to see myself as that girl that got dumped in the dirt in Golden Gate Park.

So at age 40, with my list created, I set out to take my seven horseback riding lessons. As I thumbed through the Yellow Pages looking for "Riding Stables," I envisioned myself riding in the Marin Headlands or along a California coastal beach—so romantic and adventurous. The Marin County phone book had four or five listings. I picked the largest, most prominent and detailed ad, which was for Baywood Canyon, or Circle V Stables, as known by locals.

Over the phone, I made arrangements to join a beginner class on Saturday mornings. "Do you want to learn to ride English or Western?" the person on the line asked. I had no idea what the difference was. "I'd recommend English," she suggested. "And we have a beginner English riding class on Saturday mornings, taught by Claudia."

When I arrived that first Saturday, I was immediately struck by the fact that I was the only adult in the class. The other riding students in my class ranged in age from about 9 to 14 years old. It was also obvious that each one of the other students had already had some riding lessons or experience. A few of the students seemed particularly adept in the saddle. My 5'7" frame was tall and awkward in their midst. I felt extremely self-conscious knowing that I stood out, first for my difference in age and size, and then for my inability and inexperience. Would the other students laugh at me? Would the instructor be able to give me what I needed or would she ignore me?

I introduced myself to Claudia, the instructor, and she took me to the barn to be paired with a horse for my first lesson. She gave me a thorough run down on all the rules at the barn, which included many of her own rules and regulations. "Students are not to do any of the tacking up for the horses. Tacking up means putting on the saddle and bridle and any other equipment. I, or a qualified assistant, will do all that. I don't want my students screwing up how the saddle and bridle are put on or adjusted," Claudia informed me. I felt relieved, since I didn't know how to tack up a horse anyway. She brought out a brown heavy-set horse whose tail, mane, and lower legs were black, and tied his halter to the hitching post. I would later learn that a horse of this coloring was called a bay. Claudia tossed a saddle up on his back and tightened the girth, the strap that ran under his belly.

My first and greatest challenge became immediately apparent. I had great difficulty getting my foot into the stirrup and myself up into the saddle from the ground. I had very little leg muscle or body strength. After leaving the teaching profession, I had been working at a desk job with computers and was not prepared for this kind of physical activity. Claudia's list of rules dictated that it was important that a rider not get assistance mounting the horse. She made it clear that no help would be offered with a leg up to boost the rider into the saddle or use of a mounting block to step up on.

With a great struggle, all the strength I could muster, and tremendous will power, I pushed and pulled myself up into the saddle. Once in the saddle, I looked down. The ground appeared to be far below. My horse had his ears pointed back and he began to twitch his tail. I nudged him with my legs. We walked over to get started in the class and joined the string of horses and riders that were going around the ring.

"Squeeze your legs to get him into a trot," called out Claudia to me from the center of the arena. I pressed my legs against the horse's sides. He moved forward much faster in a bumpy movement, and I began to bounce up and down in the saddle. "Post the trot. Rise up out of the saddle in your horse's rhythm," Claudia instructed.

During the following weekly lessons, once in the saddle, I progressed in balancing myself better both in the walk and in the trot. I began to feel the rhythm and was able to rise up in tune to the horse's movement. My legs ached for the few days after our lesson, but I was also getting much stronger. When I was in the saddle on the back of the horse, I didn't think about anything other than what was happening at that moment. I couldn't daydream. I couldn't concern myself with my job, my friends, or my daily routine. Horseback riding took my complete concentration. Also, this focus was fueled by fear that I might fall off and get hurt. But there were those thrilling moments when I felt connected to the horse, when I communicated to him what I wanted and he responded to my signals and me. No doubt, I came upon these moments accidentally, but I did feel them, however brief they were.

When I watched the 12-year-olds easily riding a canter, the gait faster than the trot, I longed to be able to do that, too. I realized that seven lessons could not possibly turn me into an equestrian and would do little toward making me a competent rider. Disillusionment clouded my lovely visions of riding.

Claudia, the riding instructor, was in her early thirties, a single mom, and a tough cookie. She taught English riding, but looked and acted like a cowgirl. She usually wore jeans and a sweatshirt, rather than riding britches and riding boots. Claudia's manner was abrupt and unpolished, but she exuded competence and seemed knowledgeable. She was much more friendly and comfortable with the school horses than with her students. Claudia became obsessed with getting me to be able to get on the horse without trouble. And, of course, without any assistance—no mounting block or fence rail for me to step on, no leg up from someone to boost me into the saddle. Her technique for teaching me to mount was to have me do it over and over and over. At one lesson, which turned out to be my last lesson with her, Claudia had me mount the horse more than ten times before we started to ride in that lesson. It wasn't getting any easier. That day, it got harder and harder, as I got tired and more upset. But she insisted that I must be able to do this to ride a horse.

Now it was late fall, almost winter. I had been taking lessons for three months, and I just couldn't do it any more, making such slow progress. If I couldn't improve more easily or faster than this, what was the point of it all? I felt that I should be able to do as well as the other students, to do what Claudia, the instructor, asked us to do. I agonized over what the other students (and sometimes their parents) must think about how poorly I did, how slowly I progressed. Did they look at me and think that I was wasting my time? Did Claudia think I was wasting her time? I had no compatriots of my own age and with similar difficulties with whom I could commiserate. After each lesson, I shuffled off in misery to consider all of my mistakes and things that I couldn't do.

I walked away from Claudia's class that fateful day wondering why I had ever come up with this idea in the first place. I was almost 41 years old. I didn't need such blows to my ego and confidence. I made a vow to keep my feet on the ground. It was late December, 1981.

Story 2
Heather Rides In

♦

(April 1982)

Heather on Duke in a Jumping Arena

During the next four months after giving up on what I thought of as "learning to ride," I had my 41st birthday. Winter morphed into a bright, but cool, spring. Many times I recalled those fleeting moments on the horse when I had felt joy and rapture: when the horse started to trot and I got into the rhythm, when I lost and regained my balance, when the horse listened and responded to my leg and hand signals. Those moments were few and far between, but they *were* there. And they had been wonderful.

I remembered how, at the end of every ride, my mind and body felt refreshed and energized. And, I later realized that this is what always happened when I rode, when I got up on the horse and had to pay attention to what I was doing, to what the horse was doing. I have heard of the great feelings of well-being and contentment that people have after they meditate or jog. Those descriptions tell exactly how I felt at the end of each ride. My body and mind felt more connected, not disjointed—a very relaxed feeling. Since the horse and riding took all my attention, I could only focus on those moments. After a few months of being away from riding, I became aware of this not being in my life. I noticed the absence of those lovely feelings of great relaxation.

I missed those moments of joy and exhilaration, those moments of communicating with the horse, of flying, of floating, of traveling on the back of an animal and feeling his movements. That was amazing, a sensation like no other. Maybe I could change my mind about giving up. Maybe I should give it another try. So once again, I went to the Yellow Pages and selected a listing under "Riding Stables," a different listing. I phoned a place in Woodacre called Dickson Ranch. The person who answered the phone told me: "We have a few instructors, all teaching English style. You can contact Heather, one of our instructors, to do an evaluation of your riding. She can then assign you to one of her classes." I immediately phoned Heather, and was scheduled for a half-hour evaluation on the following Saturday morning.

On that next Saturday, I headed out Sir Francis Drake Boulevard to Woodacre early so that I would find my way to Dickson Ranch and be there in plenty of time. My heart was pounding. My mouth was dry. Would I even be able to get on? After parking my car along one of the dusty lanes near two outdoor arenas, I saw an older, heavy-set woman leaning against the fence and inquired where I would find Heather.

"Oh, just wait by the picnic tables over there. She'll be along soon." Ten minutes after the scheduled time, a fair-haired woman of slight build, seeming to be in her late 20's, walked up, leading a sturdy reddish-brown horse. "I'm Heather. Are you Katherine?" "I can't get on!" I blurted out. She handed me the reins and pointed to a wooden bench at a picnic table just to our left. "Well, use that bench to get up on Stormy and come over to the arena just beyond." She turned away and walked toward the arena.

Stormy, unlike his name would have you believe, was steady and quiet. I climbed up on the picnic bench, grabbed tightly to a hunk of his mane, and easily swung my leg over his back. What a relief to be in the saddle. Once astride, I wiggled around to get comfortable. I tried to remember all or anything that I had learned under Claudia's tutelage. Stormy's girth was round and full. I felt solid and comfortable up on his back. I gave him a little squeeze with my legs. He walked slowly toward the arena. Stormy didn't act like he was in any hurry to get on with it. His movements seemed a bit reluctant. I identified with this and became aware of my anxious anticipation of what would come next.

Heather had Stormy and me ride in a circle at one end of the arena. "Kick him into a trot. He can be pretty slow, and may need some encouragement." I squeezed my legs against his sides. "Don't let Stormy push you around." I kicked him gently with my heels. "Keep him moving." I kicked again, a little harder. "Change your direction." I pulled his nose around with the right rein. "Back to a walk." I pulled on both reins.

My inner thighs began to ache from the unfamiliar stretch and tension, a feeling I hadn't had in months and had never really gotten used to in the first place. "You're doing fine," said Heather. "I have a class on Sunday mornings that you can join. And Stormy looks like a good match for you." I forgot my vow to quit this insane idea, and decided that I could change my mind about giving up.

That next Sunday morning as I headed out to Dickson Ranch, I worried: "Will I be able to get on? Will Heather give me grief about it? And then what?" When I arrived, the horses were still in their stalls. Three young teenagers were sitting on one of the tack boxes. Heather was bringing saddles and bridles out from the tack room, and setting them next to the stall doors of each of the horses. "Before you put the saddle on," said Heather, "you will all need to groom your horse and clean his hooves. Here are curry combs and hoof picks. I'll show you the best way to do it." I was surprised at first, but immediately looked forward to learning how to groom the horse assigned to me and prepare him for riding.

After suggestions and demonstrations from Heather and from the more experienced students, I began brushing Stormy's coat, mane, and tail. I could tell that he liked this. He stood very still, wiggling his ears ever so slightly. My concerns about how I would do when it was time to get on the horse abated as I fussed over Stormy and focused my attention on his needs and pleasures. "Tighten the girth just enough to keep it from slipping. Don't make it uncomfortable for your horse. Leave a space of four fingers under the cheek strap of the bridle when you buckle it," suggested Heather. She reached over to one of the horses, took hold of the bridle, and showed us exactly what she was talking about.

I always tried to arrive at class before Heather. I wanted plenty of time to get Stormy from his stall, tack him up, and head over to the picnic table to mount. When Heather was ready to start the class, I was up on Stormy, and we were warming up at the walk around the arena. Heather was usually busy getting out equipment from the tack room or briefly talking with parents. She may not have noticed my mounting technique. She never made an issue of getting on with assistance. After a few months, I came over to Heather at the end of one of our lessons and confessed: "I'm still using the picnic bench to get on." "Oh, here, let me show you another way," Heather cheerfully offered. "Just lengthen the stirrup on the near side, the horse's left side. That will make it much easier. Once you're in the saddle, just shorten up the stirrup leather."

In a flash, Heather had brushed away my faulty conviction that someone else's rule could not be broken. I had never questioned Claudia's methods and rules. I had never even considered that there might be other ways of doing things, in particular, mounting the horse. All of a sudden, I realized that I could take what worked for me, and discard what didn't. From then on, I lowered the stirrup on the near side, and had no trouble getting up. My leg and arm muscles got continuously stronger and more capable. Stormy and I never went back to the picnic table bench.

Story 3
So What If I Ride Badly

✦

(October 1982)

On Duke in Outdoor Arena at Circle V Stables

I continued my weekly riding lessons with Heather at Dickson Ranch in Woodacre for almost a year. No doubt I had made some significant progress in my riding. I was more balanced at the trot and always got the correct diagonal by rising when the horse's outside leg was going forward. And I was getting the canter and staying at that gait as long as needed. But I was still at a much lower level than her other students. Most of the students were under 16 years old, and certainly more athletic. There were now a few adults in my age range who also trained with Heather. Having ridden as children, they were trying to pick up where they left off. I saw an innate confidence in them that I lacked. Heather didn't need to give much explanation or instruction on what they needed to do for the horse to respond with the right movement. The other students got things easily and progressed quickly. I constantly wondered if I could ever catch up.

Since I had been riding with Heather, I had come to admire her talents as a horsewoman and as a teacher. I had watched her many times climb on and take the reins of a misbehaving horse and have him back doing his job in short order. She knew what each horse was capable of and what she wanted of him. Heather was able to communicate this to the horse with quick corrections and enthusiastic praise. She could also determine exactly what each student needed and provide appropriate and beneficial sugges-tions. If something didn't work, she would adapt an instruction to fit the individual. I developed great admiration for her and wished I could be one of the better students, to earn her praise and affection. I wanted to be able to do exactly what she asked of the horse and of me. And I longed to ride as well as she did.

Learning something new, trying to learn something new, particularly a physical activity that is developed through building muscle memory and requires reflexive reactions, was clearly more difficult for me as an adult. It must be for most adults. I was not very good starting out. There were no fans on the sidelines cheering me on. I might have stamina and a persistent nature, but how could I know when to pat myself on the back? I found that a good teacher could help with all of this.

I came to realize that a good teacher, observing both horse and rider from the ground, was critical to the learning process for horseback riding. The riding teacher must train the student how to physically communicate with the horse, an extremely instinctive and sensitive animal. The instructor might be able to easily perform a movement herself with the horse. But to then analyze it and describe it for someone else to understand and follow is quite amazing. And all this from the ground. Heather was aware of the rider's needs. If her instructions were not working for someone, she might get up on the horse herself to demonstrate a movement and try to give a better verbal description to the student.

One day in our group lesson as we trotted our horses around the arena, we were instructed to have the horse go into a canter on the correct lead, with the horse's inside (in relation to the circle we were on) front leg leading. Heather emphasized to us the importance of this, that the horse was much better balanced in a turn or circle with this lead. With the correct lead on the curve of a circle, the horse can make the maneuver smoothly and not lose his balance. All of Heather's school horses had been trained to pick up the correct lead in both directions. I knew how to put my outside leg back and press against the horse's side behind the girth and scoop with my butt to signal to the horse to pick up the canter and take that lead. The students trotted counter-clockwise around the arena, in single file. "Sit the trot. Outside leg back. Now, scoop your butt, and canter," Heather called. "If you're sure you've got the correct lead, just get into your horse's canter rhythm. If you're not sure your horse is leading with that front leg toward the inside of the circle, lean forward and look down at his inside front leg."

As we circled the arena, I slid my outside leg back against Stormy's side. Stormy went into the canter. His movements felt uneven and bumpy. I grabbed hold of a hunk of his mane and leaned forward over his left shoulder. He had the wrong lead. "Katherine, bring him back to a good trot and go again." I sat back, tightened my shoulders and butt. Stormy shifted his gait back down into a trot.

"You can help his balance. Just pull his nose a little to the inside with the reins as you move your leg back on the outside," Heather called to me. I could feel my stomach tighten. My legs gripped Stormy's sides, pinching me up out of the saddle. I silently told myself to relax. I pulled his nose to the inside with the reins, and moved my outside leg back to give him the signal to canter. I tried to wiggle the whip to catch his eye with it, hoping that some threat might add greater incentive to do it the way he had been trained. Stormy lunged forward into the canter. The movement felt uneven and uncomfortable. I leaned over and looked down. He had the wrong lead again. How could that be? It seemed like I was doing everything that I needed to do to get it? Why couldn't I get him to pick up the correct lead?

When the lesson was over, I rode Stormy back to his paddock, feeling as discouraged as I had ever felt about anything in my life. What a bust I was at this! How could I develop muscle memory if I never got it right in the first place? Heather hadn't asked me to quit the class, and she was certainly giving me my money's worth. But maybe it was just a matter of time, a short time, before she would tell me I should just forget about it and stop coming to the barn for lessons. I had gotten it into my head that learning to ride was a good idea, and, whenever I had tried to ignore such ideas, they just kept haunting me. I hoped that ultimately persistence and tenacity would pay off.

In that moment, the message was loud and clear. I wanted to keep doing this. I wanted to learn to ride, whatever it took. Yes, I was feeling horribly discouraged, but I liked riding, or enough parts of it, to keep going. I wasn't very good at it. I certainly wasn't a natural athlete. I didn't seem to have much of that innate ability that, with practice, would lead me to being a competent rider. It was when I compared myself to how the others were doing, or worried about how awful I must seem to someone I admired, that I felt so bad.

Well, so what if I was lousy? Who cared anyway? I was doing something that I wanted to do, and I was having a pretty good time, all in all. Damn it, I paid my money, so I deserved to get my lessons. If Heather kicked me out, there would surely be someone else who would try to teach me how to ride. "If it's worth doing, it's worth doing—even badly." So what if I rode badly?

Story 4
The Left Brain Rules

✦

(June 1983)

With Duke at Circle V Stables

I began to discover that competent horseback riding requires being both athletic and intuitive. If you have to think consciously, to reason logically, about what you need to do to have the horse listen and follow your instructions, it's too late. You could find yourself nose down in the dirt, as I have done many times. Riding a horse with confidence and control comes from developing innate abilities through practice until you find that place where you communicate reflexively, without thinking about it, with your horse. The rider must build muscle memory and rely on immediate non-verbal actions. This is a team sport like no other. Horses are instinctive and sensitive animals and can respond to very subtle cues.

From what I have observed of others and experienced myself, the more capable and talented horseback riders have more of that innate ability and have built muscle memory and know how to use it. As for myself up to the age of 40, I had leaned heavily on the logical side, the left side of my brain. I had not developed my right brain abilities and lacked the spontaneous muscle memory needed to deal effectively with the actions and responses of a horse. For me to develop an ability to sense instantly what was needed, I formed ways to get to that reflexive place through practice and repetition.

Growing up in my family, logic and analysis were valued and encouraged. Until I began horseback riding, I had spent my time in activities that were developed through logical techniques and methodical principles. My father was an attorney-at-law, who supported the family and dominated the household. My sister, three years my senior, had, early in high school, tested close to genius. She proved her special talents in math, science, and debate, going all through Stanford University on a full scholarship. Left-brain qualities were praised and encouraged in our family, with my sister as the ultimate model to follow. Accomplishments in creative activities such as sports and the arts were ridiculed and made fun of, as if lesser brainpower was needed for such endeavors. My high school curriculum path was College Prep. Though I exhibited some talent in drawing and painting, my father frowned on art classes. I never included them in my formal course study before I was in college and out on my own.

For me to react instantly to the horse with the appropriate signal or response, without conscious thought, first I had to memorize what movement was needed for a particular situation. I would silently repeat to myself what I had to do over and over. After what seemed like a thousand attempts, I could take hold of it. When I wobbled off balance in the saddle, my instinct was to lean forward and grab the horse around the neck—the worst thing I could do. "Sit back. Sit up in the saddle directly on your seat bones. You'll be more balanced and slow him if he's rushing," were Heather's instructions. "Your upright and balanced position in the saddle will steady the horse and help get and keep the correct rhythm," elaborated Heather. If I followed these instructions and not my automatic responses, it worked.

Developing my right-brain abilities built my confidence. I learned to rely on my intuitive reactions. It forced me to focus on the immediate moment, would not allow me to be distracted or sidetracked. It required all of me. Any alternative was to risk serious injury and pain. Horseback riding offered nothing more than what I got at that moment. The rewards were the enjoyment of the moment, an invaluable lesson for me.

I would never be a major competitor, or even a minor competitor, in the equestrian show ring. I could not look to pursuing a career in the horse world, as a rider, as an instructor, or as a trainer. I could only focus on mastering the immediate movement, which came through memorization and repetition. Ultimately, I hoped I could master not having to think about what I was doing, that I would rise to the level of unconscious competence.

I had been riding under Heather's guidance for about two years, and had long since realized that my early plan of seven lessons to competence was ridiculous. The idea of having my own horse was more regularly creeping into my thoughts. Stormy, one of Heather's school mounts, was still a great ride for me, particularly on the trail. If I wanted to try some low-level jumping or expand my dressage skills with more intricate gaits and movements, I would need a different horse and probably my own horse. I started to think beyond my present level and to look to building greater capabilities.

"Let's go out for a nice relaxing trail ride, just have some fun," suggested Heather to her students one early Sunday morning. We headed off on a leisurely trail ride up into the hills above Woodacre. There were five of us in all that day—Heather in the lead, then Laura and John, me in second to last in the string of horses, and Patrick, bringing up the rear. "We'll start off with a good run up Drake's Hill. Just get your heels down, grab some mane, and lean slightly forward," Heather called back to us. It was an amazing rush. We all knew, riders and horses, that this was a fun dash to get some energy out and experience the exhilaration of speed. Going uphill in this position had minimal risk of injury or harm for a maximum thrill. "Yahoo," hollered Patrick as his horse tried to overtake the others, but soon slowed back to a trot. By the time we had reached the summit of this low hill, everyone was back to a trot. Horses and riders were happy to be able to catch their breath.

The riders fell back into their position in line. Heather led us along a beautiful trail, lined with oaks and lush shrubbery. I was relaxed and comfortable, not worrying about what I needed to do to make Stormy behave. He followed along calmly and securely in his spot in the string of horses. Where the trail straightened out, Heather would signal to us and we would change gait up into a trot. Then back to a walk where the trail would twist and turn or drop downhill.

"Help. Yikes. Ouch. Ouch. Damn it," came from directly behind me. Stormy lurched forward as Patrick's horse came galloping past us with Patrick hanging on his neck. "Bees. Bees. Bees. There are bees all over us. Ouch. Ouch. Help." Patrick's horse made a small leap into the air, spun around, and then headed in another direction. Patrick continued on in the same direction and went flying into the bushes.

Stormy charged forward and trotted nervously up the trail. I started my mantra, the one I had memorized for just such a moment. To myself: *"Heels down. Sit up. Sit up. Leg on. Move him forward, into your hand. Keep him going forward, but into the walk."* As my stomach lurched and my balance wavered, I kept repeating these instructions to myself. I concentrated my whole being on listening to myself and following what I was saying the best I could. Over and over and over. Stormy slowed to a steady walk. He became calm and collected. Heather shot past us at a gallop, heading down the trail. "Just stay there. I'll go for Patrick's horse," she called out to us.

Patrick stood up and brushed himself off. The bees seemed to have been frightened as well, and were no longer in pursuit of him, even though he had disturbed their hive. I sat on Stormy as he leaned his head down to nibble on some grass. A vision of Stormy galloping down the trail along with the other horse flashed in my head. That hadn't happened. I had put my heels down, sat up on him, and moved him forward into a walk. My mantra hadn't come directly from the right side of my brain, but I had reacted in a way that put me in control and out of harm's way. I let out a huge sigh of relief as we saw Heather riding back up the trail, leading the riderless horse.

"Let's head back to the barn. I think we have had our ride for today," Heather commented. She turned to go back down the trail. As she changed directions and passed by me, I heard her mutter quietly, "So much for a nice, relaxing trail ride."

Maybe I would ultimately get past the logical and burn through to the intuitive. For me to build muscle memory and skills to immediately communicate with the horse, I had to start with memorizing on the left side of the brain and keep repeating it until the right side took hold of it, until my body memorized it, not just my mind. I had to practice doing the movement until I built muscle memory that I could call up at any time.

Story 5
My First Horse is a Duke

◆

(April 1984)

Duke Showing Off Soon After Arriving at Circle V Stables

Cactus got me thinking about getting my own horse. Cactus was a 12-year-old gelding Quarter horse used as a school horse by Cathy, one of the other two riding instructors at Circle V Stables in Fairfax. Cactus was known as a solid citizen around the barn. He was being put up for sale. Cactus was a popular ride with the students because of his mellow manner and good behavior.

That previous fall, Heather had moved her riding school operation and all of her students from Dickson Ranch to Circle V Stables. She taught the older children and beginner and intermediate adults. Cathy taught the younger children, and Larry taught the advanced riders in the hunter-jumper discipline. I had seen Cactus in the ring during lessons and had admired how steady and reliable he was. When Heather passed along to her students that Cathy was going to sell him, I thought how great it would be to have my own horse—particularly a solid and reliable Quarter horse who seemed to have no bad habits.

Typically, school horses developed bad habits, from putting up with inexperienced riders all the time. Having your own horse and then getting assistance in training could make a lot of difference in how your ride behaved. I knew that Quarter horses were bred for their reliable and calm dispositions. They had a reputation for being good trail horses and fast for short sprints. From what I had read and seen, Quarter horses preferred to take it easy rather than cause trouble—a good match for a green, inexperienced rider.

As I thought more about it, I began to thrill at the idea of having my own horse, not having to share with the other students. I could come and ride any time I wanted. Wouldn't that be wonderful! Buying and having all my own tack equipment, saddle and bridle, also began to dominate my thoughts. These images conjured up all those earlier romantic and adventuresome daydreams of galloping along a coastal beach or of ambling through the hills dotted with oak trees.

The school horse that I usually rode at this time was an Appaloosa named Aggie. Similar to the Quarter horse, Appaloosas were bred to provide a solid and reliable ride, without any surprises. But Aggie was also a cranky, obstinate mare, who needed constant reminders of who was the boss. Since I continually wondered if I was up to being the boss, Aggie took advantage. If she didn't want any of it on a particular day, Aggie would kick out to the side and just about dump me (or any other of her riders) off. It always had the effect she wanted: I got scared and backed down from whatever I was asking her to do. The idea of having my own horse, who was ready, willing, and able, grew quickly into an obsession. Every time Aggie tried to put me in my place (of the lower order) or dump me off, I flashed on that image of my own horse that was obedient, calm, and quick to respond to my every request.

Most of the school horses had little quirks and problems like Aggie had. Inexperienced students, such as myself, couldn't help but reinforce these problems. I began thinking that, if I had control over the horse's training and riding with Heather's help, no such problems would develop. Heather could work with the horse and train the horse properly. I relied on the hope that she could teach me how to keep the horse from getting away with misbehaviors.

I knew that buying a horse was not exactly practical. A horse required a different kind of care than a dog or a cat needed. And being a responsible horse owner had monetary obligations and considerations. It wasn't just the purchase price that could be costly. The owner's responsibilities included monthly board and care fees, regular vet checks, and the necessary visits from a farrier for shoeing every six weeks or so. When I brought up the idea with Heather, she responded with enthusiasm. In fact, this marked a major change in my relationship with Heather. We both realized that my commitment to riding was long term and sincere, no matter what the trials and tribulations. I was not in it for just the seven lessons.

"If you're thinking about Cactus, I suggest that you can do better than that, and for just about the same money, or less. Certainly a Quarter horse would be a breed we would want to consider for you. Maybe a younger gelding that has more athletic ability. I'll check around," said Heather. I rushed home to look at my bank account balance and all available monetary resources. My excitement overshadowed any of the practical considerations.

Each week Heather had something to report on possible horse-buying opportunities, but nothing concrete developed. We would hear of some friend of a friend who had a horse for sale, but, when we checked it out, the price was way out of my range, or the horse was too green (untrained and inexperienced), or too young, or not a breed that would work best for me at this point. Heather outlined for me that, for my first horse, my chances for success were better with such breeds as a Quarter horse or an Appaloosa. These horse breeds have reputations for being solid and more predictable and so usually work better for the less-experienced rider. I also had to consider that, if the horse already had a lot of training, the price could well be out of line with my budget (and capabilities).

Then one day Heather came over to me at the beginning of our lesson and said: "A friend of Pamela's mentioned that there's a 5-year-old Quarter horse for sale at a western training barn in Sonoma. It might be worth checking out. I'll call and, if it sounds good, maybe we could go take a look." I was glad that Heather would be initiating the inquiry and asking the questions. She would know how to kick the tires.

The following week, Heather and I were on our way to see this Quarter horse. The owners of the training facility ran a Western riding operation and regularly assisted clients and friends in buying and selling horses. "His name is Duke, and he has lots of training and experience as a trail horse," explained the barn manager as he pointed to the third stall down the row. As we walked toward the stall, a big chestnut-colored head popped out of the open upper half of the stall door. Heather turned to the barn manager and began her questions. I reached into my pocket for the apple I had brought along. Duke leaned his head farther out and grabbed the apple. I admired his large, intelligent-looking eyes, his soft reddish-brown coat, and his stocky build. He seemed strong, well muscled, and in excellent health. He sure looked good to me, definitely must be a great buy. But from Heather's tone as she talked to the fellow and looked Duke over, I wasn't so sure she felt the same way.

We needed to take a test drive. So Duke was tacked up with saddle and bridle and taken into the arena for us to ride. Heather hopped up into the saddle and did some walk and trot. She nodded her head, as if in approval of how he went, and dismounted. I put my foot into the stirrup, grabbed a hunk of his mane, and hoisted myself up. Duke seemed perfect to me. Not too tall, but tall enough for my size and build. He looked to be about 16.2 hands high. (Horses' sizes are measured in hands with a hand being 4 inches.) Duke was calm and steady as we set off at a walk. I nudged him into a trot and circled around the arena. He didn't rush and his trot was rhythmic and easy to post. Duke must be the perfect horse for me, I told myself.

As Heather and I walked back to the car, Heather commented, "Let's think about this. The price is too high for the kind of training and experience Duke has. Maybe we can do better for you." My heart sank. I bit my tongue. All I could think about was Duke and how great it would be to have him as my riding companion. This Quarter horse just seemed so perfect, though I didn't have much to compare him to. So far, my rides had been seasoned school horses, who had lots of experience and some training in English riding with dressage and stadium jumping. Duke had probably never even had an English saddle on his back or a snaffle bit in his mouth.

Three days went by and not a word from Heather's direction. I decided to phone the training facility, find out if Duke was still for sale. If so, I could offer them a lower price. Maybe Heather would be more enthusiastic if I got the price down. Yes, Duke was still there. He had not yet been sold. Would they take a few hundred dollars less for him? No, the price was firm.

Another three days went by. Maybe there would not be another horse as good as Duke that would come our way soon. I was paying the bill, so I would be making the ultimate decision. I decided that, if he were still for sale, I would pay the full price. First, I phoned Heather to let her know what I wanted to do. She was out and I left her a message. I wanted this horse. I was willing to pay the price. I wanted Heather to work with him, with me, to teach us as much as she could. I called the barn manager at the training facility. I felt lightheaded as I dialed the number to then confirm my offer and make arrangements to pick up Duke.

"You can bring a check when you come to pick him up," the barn manager assured me. "Okay, look for us on Saturday around noon, unless you hear back from me otherwise," I replied. Heather had an old two-horse trailer that she used in transporting students and horses. She had sounded more resigned than enthusiastic when I talked to her about getting Duke. Somehow I just knew Heather would and could help me make it work. As we headed up to Sonoma that Saturday with the trailer hitched to Heather's truck, Heather briefed me about what we could expect from him the first few months.

"As soon as I get him into a training routine, we'll have you doing lots of transitions from walk to trot, trot to canter, and back again. I want to be sure he understands and can do what is expected of him for a movement," Heather outlined. "Duke is used to Western equipment and artificial aids, as spurs and such, to keep him in line. We will be asking him to listen by using *natural* aids, as leg and voice commands." Her plan sounded fun and exciting and reliable to me. I could hear Duke in the trailer, shifting around to get his balance as we drove back to Fairfax. At that moment, I found it hard to concentrate on the practical plan outlined for his training.

Story 6
Break A Leg

✦

(May 1984)

With My Right Leg in a Cast

Now I had my very own horse. I wasn't fourteen years old, but forty some-thing. I could hardly believe it. I daydreamed about being able to ride out on the trail whenever I wanted, of building such rapport with this animal that my will would be his will. I had no clear picture of what it would take to get to that place. Whatever had gotten me this far surely would take me to the next wondrous plateau. I knew that I could count on Heather to keep us going in the right direction, and keep us alive and out of harm's way.

Duke was quite a handsome Quarter horse. His chestnut red coat shone after he was groomed. His head and neck had that classic Quarter horse look, compact and muscled. Duke had been trained as a trail and pack horse and had lots of experience in these endeavors, according to his previous owners. He looked quite fit and was in his prime at five years old—young enough to learn some dressage and jumping, old enough to have settled down.

With all the grooming skills I had learned from Heather, I had no trouble getting Duke ready for our lessons. His ground manners were good. I suspected his Western training had probably included "minding his manners with the ladies." Duke's "good ole boy" personality showed itself from the start. He took things as they came to him, and seemed to do what was in his best interest. And Duke wasn't interested in causing any trouble when he was being fussed over and groomed. He loved that kind of attention.

Our first month in the barn at Circle V Stables was uneventful. Duke had to stay in a restricted area in quarantine for two weeks as a precaution against bringing anything into the barn that was contagious. Then he was moved into his permanent stall, where he could fraternize nose-to-nose with the other geldings in the adjacent stalls. Heather scheduled us for weekly one-hour private lessons. We used the saddle and bridle of one of her school horses. Heather started us off with basic exercises in the walk and in the trot, with focus on keeping a steady rhythm and good balance.

I didn't feel fearful on Duke's back. We were doing exercises and movements that I was familiar with, and he seemed pretty mellow and easy to handle. I wasn't about to do any riding without Heather around until I felt confident that I knew what to expect and could handle it. At the finish of our third lesson, Heather came over to me: "Let's take him out on a trail ride on Saturday. He will certainly like that, being the seasoned trail horse he is." I was ecstatic. My dream was coming true. That wonderful romantic scene of me on my horse galloping through the hills, in harmony with nature and life!

That Friday evening, I drove out to the barn after work to spend time getting Duke's tack and equipment ready for the next day's adventure. Early the next morning, I suited up with helmet and boots. I didn't have leather boots yet but pulled on my rubber knee-high paddock boots without concern. The weather couldn't have been better that morning. While I groomed and saddled Duke, Heather tacked up one of her school horses. Off we went.

As part of Heather's riding program, she regularly took her students out on school horses for trail rides up on the hiking and riding trails behind Circle V Stables. I had been on a few of these treks, and was familiar with the territory. The main trail was a fire road that was wide enough for two or three horses abreast. This trail meandered around the hillsides and was fairly level. A number of forks in the road offered a variety of alternate routes, with gradual inclines and narrow winding riding paths.

Directly behind Circle V Stables was a steep access road that connected to the fire road. "Get your heels down, grab a hunk of his mane, and kick him into a good trot," instructed Heather. She stayed out in front and we trotted up the hill. Duke was energetic and kept the brisk pace. As I had learned from a number of times in this same sort of terrain, going up a hill was a great way to get a rush, a flying feeling on the horse, but staying solid in the saddle. It was hard to be dislodged in this position—heels down, weight slightly forward, horse controlled by gravity. The horse got tired before long and was easy to slow down. Duke was true to his breed, with a quick burst of energy at the startup. He soon slowed down to take it easy. He seemed happy to enjoy a brief moment of speed and then settle down to an easier pace.

Once up on to the fire road, we ambled along at a comfortable walk. I felt the warmth on my back from the morning sun and the gentle rolling movement of the horse under me. I could look out over the beautiful hills of West Marin. When we had straight stretches, Heather would give me a heads up and we would trot these distances. Duke's trot was fairly comfortable. I could easily rise up out of the saddle in his rhythm and post his trot. I had no trouble staying up with Heather and felt relaxed, without any panic or fear. Just like Heather had predicted, Duke was enjoying being out on the trail.

As we rounded a bend and the road straightened out for some distance, Heather called back to me: "Let's canter this stretch before we turn around to head home." She signaled to her horse for the next upward gait and went into an easy canter. Duke immediately rallied to the cue, not wanting to be left behind. We were off. We were flying along the trail. My stomach tightened up and my breathing shortened. For a few minutes, the feeling of speed and the pounding of what seemed like thundering hoofs were exhilarating, unbelievably exciting. I bounced up and down in the saddle. With each stride Duke took, the distance between the saddle and me became greater. The impact back into the saddle as I came down became harder. Suddenly I flew into the air and landed on the hard dirt road.

As I hit the ground, I felt a gigantic jolt and a sharp pain up my right leg. For a moment, I was stunned. I didn't know exactly what had happened or where I was. But Duke knew that the fun was over. He slowed and came to a halt with the reins dangling over his neck. I could hear Heather: "Are you okay?" I couldn't answer and just lay there for a few minutes, collecting my thoughts and myself. I pushed myself up and walked slowly over to Duke. The pain in my leg was getting worse, but I knew that, no matter what, I had to get myself back up into the saddle. I couldn't walk back to the barn and would have to ride.

Heather rode over to us as I grabbed hold of the reins dangling around Duke's neck. Even though it hurt like hell, I pushed and pulled myself up into the saddle. At least I could do that. No blood or bones were showing. Heather and I turned the horses toward home and rode back to the barn at the walk.

I took off Duke's saddle and bridle and brushed his back. My body felt jarred, and my leg was now numb. As soon as Duke was settled in his stall and a few carrots had been dropped into his feed bucket, I headed home for a hot bath and a glass of wine.

The next morning the phone rang before I was out of bed. As I rolled over to answer, a throbbing pain shot up my right side. "Hello?" "Katherine, how are you? I've been worrying that maybe you got hurt more than you thought yesterday." "Oh, Heather. Yikes, you might be right. My leg is killing me. Let me see how things look and I'll call you back later." As I put down the receiver, I knew that Heather was right. My leg was twice its normal size and I could barely walk to the bathroom. I slowly and carefully got dressed and headed for the Emergency Room of a nearby hospital.

By the time X-rays had been taken and I was back on the doctor's examining table, I could no longer put any weight onto my right foot and leg. The doctor held up the X-ray for me and pointed out a hairline fracture. "The cast will need to go up past your knee, so that there is minimal movement for healing. You can expect to keep it on for about 6 weeks."

As the nurse began to swab alcohol on my leg and prepare the cast materials, big tears rolled down my cheeks. I had my own horse, but would not be able to ride. "What a colossal injustice," I thought. What lesson did I learn from this adventure? I was feeling blue and wondered how long it would be before I was back up in the saddle.

Story 7
The Right Equipment Matters

✦

(July 1984)

Riding in the Indoor Ring at Circle V Stables

"Katherine, you need to get a snaffle bit for Duke, and some riding boots for yourself. Probably field boots," outlined Heather. The cast had been removed from my leg two weeks earlier, and Duke and I were back to our regular lesson routine. But I hadn't done anything yet about getting proper boots. "And you will need side reins pretty soon, so we can do some ground work on the lunge line with Duke," Heather added. "Take the catalog of equipment for horse and rider from my tack box to look through to get some ideas. Offutt's in Petaluma should have what you need." As I reached for the thick and rumpled riding equipment catalog, I hoped that all the things Heather had been talking about would be clearly pictured and described so that I would have no trouble getting exactly what we needed.

Saddles, bridles, bits, saddle pads, boots, leg wraps. Dressage saddle, jumping saddle, close contact saddle, all-purpose saddle, eventing saddle. Girths, leathers, stirrups, halters. Double bridle, dropped noseband bridle, rolled flash bridle, snaffle bridle, figure-8 bridle. Snaffle bit, D-ring snaffle bit, curb bit, eggbutt snaffle, kimberwicke, jointed rubber pelham. Bell boots, splint boots, front boots, hind boots, shipping boots. And these are just for the horse. Riding boots, field boots, paddock boots. Breeches, jodhpurs, chaps, half-chaps. Schooling whip, dressage whip, jumping whip, crop. I had heard the names of many of the pieces of riding equipment, but did not have a clear picture of what most of them were or how they were used.

Up until now, I had concentrated only on the basics of what I needed, of what the horse needed. As I thumbed through the catalog, I realized that there was a huge body of knowledge on the equipment used to train and ride a horse. I could also see a variety of disciplines and styles existed, each with its own philosophy and associated tack requirements.

After the disaster of getting dumped in the dirt when we had been out on a trail ride, I knew that I had to get some good equipment for myself, starting with leather boots. Thank goodness I had been wearing one of the riding helmets from the student tack box on that fateful day. But my rubber paddock boots had no support, and were unfortunately not adequate protection for my lower legs and ankles. I had overheard some of the other students talking enthusiastically about Offutt's Tack Shop in Petaluma and decided to go up for a shopping trip. A pair of good leather riding boots was top priority. I would also want to invest in riding breeches and proper socks to fit the boots and breeches. I was still using Heather's schooling equipment—saddle and bridle—for Duke. I knew that I had to get tack for him, but that would have to come later.

It all seemed so easy and fun, going shopping. Carefully following the directions, I drove to the outskirts of the west side of Petaluma. I came to the entrance road to Offutt's. A large worn and battered sign was posted at the street entrance. A one-lane dirt road led to a two-story, wood framed house. I drove along and around to what seemed to be the back of the house. "PARK HERE" was posted along a fence adjacent to the old house. A large black Lab dozed by the side of a porch with a screen door. As I stepped onto the porch and reached to open the screen door, voices came from inside. "What size saddle do you need? Regular or wide tree? How much padding for the knee rolls? Will you want leathers, stirrups, and a girth?" My mouth went dry and my stomach tightened as I listened to the conversations. The language being spoken was foreign to me.

Shouldn't I know all about this by now? I had been taking lessons for more than two years. Inadequacy overwhelmed me. How could I get what I needed? I didn't know what questions to ask. I didn't know the terminology. I didn't know anything about sizes for horse equipment. An irrational feeling of panic took over. I couldn't stop it.

As I looked around the main room, the shelves bulged with a great variety of items, some strange and unusual, a few familiar. Leather, metal, and cloth equipment hung from racks. Saddles, bridles, saddle pads, horse blankets, helmets, breeches went from floor to ceiling. Three separate open doorways went off into other rooms that looked just as full. Two women were standing by a large desk, comparing an array of bridles. I surmised that the older woman in jeans and a cotton shirt must be the proprietor or a sales person. She was explaining the benefits and drawbacks of the features for one of the bridles. Behind her hung another fifty or more bridles and parts of bridles from hooks on a wall rack.

I scurried past the two women and into one of the adjoining rooms. I did not want to draw attention to myself or attract any questions as to what I was looking for. At least not yet, not until I had the lay of the land. In the next room, a large part of one wall displayed what I calculated must be hundreds of bits, in all sorts of configurations, of varying sizes. I scanned the metal and rubber mouthpieces hanging from their side rings, hoping to recognize the types that were used on the bridles for Heather's school horses and for Duke. I could hardly believe how many different variations of designs and sizes were on display. What determined the type of bit you were supposed to use? Did they come in different sizes? How did you measure that?

Beyond the wall of bits were shelves packed with boxes that displayed pictures of riding boots, some high topped, some low topped, some with laces, some with zippers. Sample boots sat on their boxes. As I moved closer, I wondered if I would ever find my way through this maze. Would I ever be able to understand the language in this foreign land? Could I even fit into any of this stuff?

I reached over and picked up a tall black leather boot without laces or a zipper. How did you get your foot into such a boot? How did you get a boot off by yourself? I flashed on a scene from an old movie that I had watched some years ago in which a young woman in complete riding attire had dismounted from her horse, sat down on a bench, and an attendant appeared. She held up her leg and the attendant took hold of each boot and pulled it off with some effort. Is that what I had to have? Someone close by who would always be there to help me get my boots off?

"Looking for dress boots? Or would you like to try on a pair of our field boots?" offered a young woman coming toward me. "We've got some boot pulls and a boot jack over by that little bench. You can use a pair of socks from that bin over there." I couldn't think of what to say to her, no clue of what questions to ask or how to ask them. I couldn't bring myself to ask:

"What are field boots? What is a boot jack? How does it work?" I felt horribly uncomfortable as a grown woman in such a store with no idea of what I was actually shopping for. "Oh, no, just looking around," I muttered and turned away. I hustled on down the row toward racks of pants that looked like leggings and seemed to be of extremely small sizes.

As I wandered aimlessly through the rows feeling quite lost, I spotted a large cabinet stuffed with books of all sizes. The book covers had such titles as *Grooming to Win, The Lungeing Book, Veterinary Notes for Horse Owners, Centered Riding, Eventing Explained.* I scanned the titles, searching for some help. *The Handbook of Riding* looked promising and helpful, as I thumbed through the pages. A little bit of everything—from preparation for riding to improving your riding, to saddlery and equipment. Ahhh, I sighed with some relief. Just what I needed. I made my way to the front of the store, paid for my book, and set off to read it from cover to cover.

That evening and for the next few days, I studied the descriptions and photos in *The Handbook of Riding.* There was just enough information to help me begin to recognize and understand the different types of bits and bridles. This handbook seemed more like an encyclopedia. There was even a page on what a stock tie was and how to tie it for different kinds of competitions. I knew that I wouldn't understand it all right away and just had to take it in a little at a time. The descriptions of equipment for the rider and tack for the horse had detailed explanations and lots of photographs.

Here was a place where it would have probably been a great advantage to be about 12 years old with a mom who would clear the path. Someone who would admit total ignorance and employ the assistance of a knowledgeable clerk to take care of her child rider. But it felt to me like there was much more at stake than just finding a pair of boots that fit and going off with them. Boots were rather expensive. I didn't want to buy the wrong thing. I didn't want to show up at a riding lesson with something completely inappropriate, then return whatever I had purchased and still have to figure out what I needed to get.

When I arrived for my lesson on Duke with Heather the next Sunday, I desperately hoped there would be no accidents. Even though I was wearing a helmet, I still had my rubber paddock boots. I tacked up Duke and headed to the outdoor arena. "Katherine, I thought I would see you all decked out from head to toe in spiffy new leather riding gear, and definitely with some high leather boots," acknowledged Heather. "Oh, Heather, I did get to Offutt's. Oh my, it was overwhelming. I hate to admit it, but I just didn't know what to buy or how to go about finding what I needed. There were so many different kinds of boots, both English and Western. And the horse tack! Yikes." Duke snorted and shifted his weight. He was being ignored and didn't like that.

"I've been meaning to get up there myself, get some new lunge lines and a new lunge whip. How 'bout if we meet up there next week and we can shop together?" Heather offered. I didn't hesitate: "That would be fantastic! I would love to treat you to lunch on such an outing." If anybody knew anything, it would be Heather. My gloom was washed away. I again felt encouraged about going shopping. "What are field boots, Heather? Is that what I should be trying on?" I can now look back upon these moments as those rites of passage that I had to go through in order to enter the great, fun place of finding just the right equipment for just the right purpose. I soon came to love decking out my horse in some special saddle pad, such as a blue one with white stars and piping.

Story 8
Heather Fashions a Whip

◆

(February 1985)

Going through a Gymnastic Set of Jumps

It was late February. Many trees and bushes were bare. For our Sunday lesson, we would be riding in the outdoor arena on this cool, bright morning. After I tacked up Duke and was in the saddle, we rode down from the upper barn at Circle V Stables to the big outdoor arena. When I got Duke the year before, I had moved from the large class lessons to private lessons with Heather. Everybody benefited. Both Duke and I could get special attention. Some days Heather zeroed in on my leg position, on my balance in the saddle, or on the amount of weight I had in holding the reins. Other days, she focused on Duke's training and behavior, on his responses to my signals to him. If he did not understand what was being asked or did not cooperate, Heather would get on. She could then clarify or make a point with Duke when I was not able to.

Duke had a "good 'ole boy" personality. I had come to know that he responded to what was in his own best interest. If Duke didn't think that he had to do something, he took it easy and didn't exert himself. And he was very much a horse of his breed, the Quarter Horse. As such, he was reliable and dependable, calm and laid back, not easily excited. Duke had lots of experience as a trail and pack horse. This, along with his herd nature, made him an expert at being able to avoid working too hard if the rider was at all reluctant or timid. When he was out on the trail with other horses, he always exerted that short-lived burst of speed at the beginning of a run, doing just what he was bred for—sprinting a quarter mile. I could always count on him to slow down soon and drop back into a calm and steady pace. In the arena, when no other horses were there to compete with him, Duke would take it slow and easy around the ring.

As we entered the arena that morning, Heather noticed: "Where's your whip? You just got knee-high boots, side reins, and a dressage whip—all that new riding gear. But I don't see one of those most critical things. You know, it's when you don't have some piece of equipment that you usually need it." It wasn't that I had to use the whip much. In fact, one of the major things that caused me difficulty was **not** using it when it was needed. I was usually hesitant about enforcing my commands. With Duke, the difference was whether I *held* a whip or not. Such a difference. When I had a whip, he saw it. That's all that was needed. His pace was bright. When I was carrying a whip, Duke was quite willing to move up to the faster gait as I gently squeezed my legs against his sides. When he realized that I didn't have a whip, he ignored me, ignored my leg, ignored my signals.

Forgetting to bring the whip could definitely cause great struggles and frustration for me. "Should I go back up to the barn and get it?" I asked. "No, not yet. Let's see how it goes. Maybe he'll have more respect for you today without it. Use a firm leg. It's important to have all the equipment that you might need. If you don't have it, and you do need it, you're sure to have trouble."

Heather started us off with some warm up exercises at the walk. Not much problem, though it took us a few times around the ring to get into the rhythm. Then Heather spelled out: "T-R-O-T." (We both knew that if she called out the gait, he would be responding to her voice command, rather than to my leg signal.) I pressed my legs to Duke's sides. Duke went into the trot, or at least, somewhat of a trot. Duke gave it the minimum of effort, barely brisker than the walk. I accentuated my movements and rose high up into my rib cage in the posting trot. He continued to plod along without any change in his gait. I kicked his sides. Duke ignored me and continued to move without energy.

"I had better go back up to the barn and get the whip," I offered. "No, no. Just hold on. I'll get one for you." Heather turned and walked to the far side of the arena, away from the gate. She hoisted herself up over the railing and ducked into the woods. A few minutes later, Heather emerged from the trees with a small, slender branch that was the perfect shape and length for a dressage whip. "Here you go," she said. She reached up and handed me the improvised whip. Duke eyed the tree branch. "T-R-O-T," Heather called. I squeezed with my legs and off we went, briskly and on the money with no hesitation. Duke carefully eyed this odd whip out of the corner of his eye. His bright pace told me that he saw it clearly. What a relief not to have to schlep up to the barn to get the whip.

At home that afternoon, I thought about how clever Heather was, how quickly she was able to come up with what was needed to make it work. My admiration for her was heightened by her skills and intuition in working with horses, working with Duke, and in teaching me. I felt satisfaction in making progress and enjoying my time in the saddle.

When I went to the bathroom and glanced at myself in the mirror early the next morning, I gasped at my reflection. My face, neck, and lower arms were ablaze with an ugly red rash. Blisters were beginning to form. My ears, neck, and cheeks throbbed and glowed red with swelling. The poison oak rash was everywhere. The itching, stinging pain had startled me awake. I realized that the whip Heather had fashioned was a branch from a poison oak bush. I am extremely allergic to poison oak.

After I phoned the Urgent Care Unit at the local hospital to get an appointment for a cortisone shot, I called Heather. "You know that wonderful whip that you fashioned for me yesterday? Well, if you don't know it already, it must have been poison oak. I'm covered with a horrible rash." "Oh, dear, I'm so sorry. I hate to tell you this, but I'm not allergic to poison oak. I could probably rub poison oak leaves all over me, and nothing would happen." As I hung up the phone and headed for the car, I reminded myself that I had better give Duke a good soapy bath right away to wash the residue off his coat.

Story 9
We Get Competitive

✦

(September 1985)

On Duke in Dressage Training Level Test at Dickson Ranch

Part of Heather's riding program for her students included participating in the horse trials competition at Dickson Ranch in Woodacre. After she had relocated to Circle V Stables, Heather trailered her students and their horses (or the school horses) to Dickson four or five times on weekends during the spring and summer months to compete in Dickson's horse shows. The Dickson Horse Trials offered a Green Division for inexperienced horses and beginner riders. This was a great opportunity for those just starting out. Most horse shows started at the next level, called Novice Level. Beginners (riders and horses) had difficulty getting some practice with show protocol, routines, and jitters. To get enough experience to compete in horse trials starting at Novice Level, a rider needed to compete at a very basic level somewhere.

The one-day horse trials competition is a shortened version of a three-day event (also called combined training) and includes the same three phases: dressage, cross-country jumping, and stadium jumping, but all done on the same day. Each phase is scored separately and offers individual ribbons. An overall, combined score is calculated to award show ribbons. A horse and rider can enter any one phase or all three. Ribbons are awarded to riders with the least number of penalty points, the lowest scores. In the dressage phase, the judges score the riders with positive points. Then the dressage scores are converted to penalty points, and the lower scores are the winning rides for that phase. In the jumping phases, riders accumulate penalty points. For overall scores, all penalty points are added up to determine the winners, those with the lowest points.

"Let's have you learn the Dressage Training Level Test I for the Green Division. It will give you a goal and an opportunity to see what we need to work on. This will highlight your weakest skills and build confidence in your strengths," Heather pointed out. I had been watching other students practicing their dressage tests. I had even gone over to Dickson Ranch a couple of times to check on their performances. So I had some idea of what she was asking. To test horse and rider competence in dressage, tests are performed at various levels with increasing difficulty of movements. A prescribed set of movements for each test must be executed. A judge (or judges) scores for such things as the exact location of where the gait change is made, the accuracy of size of circles (20 meters, 15 meters, etc.), the correct lead in the canter, and so forth.

While my father valued logic and science and encouraged his children in left-brain activities, my mother had gently shoved us into the performing arts. In my pre-teen years, she had enrolled me in The Gentry Sisters' School of Dance and Drama on Clement Street in San Francisco. Twice a week for many years, I had taken tap dancing, ballet, and drama lessons. The Gentry Sisters encouraged their students to perform in front of an audience and regularly held recitals. I hoped that this early introduction to performing would now pay off. Memorizing and performing a series of riding movements appealed to me and to my logical mind, that overactive left side of my brain. Though I never enjoyed the heat of battle—entering into competition—my theatrical side secretly thrilled at the idea of performing, hopefully well, in front of an audience.

The following Sunday, Heather handed me a sheet of paper with a large rectangular pattern printed on it, letters at different points around the pattern, and circular dotted lines crisscrossing within the rectangle. Official instructions of the movements for horse and rider were outlined below the diagram. "You and Duke will be working on the pattern for Dressage Training Level Test I. It will be fun. Then you can enter the Dickson Trials, just the dressage phase. A test can show where you need work and can reveal your strengths. You will surprise yourself."

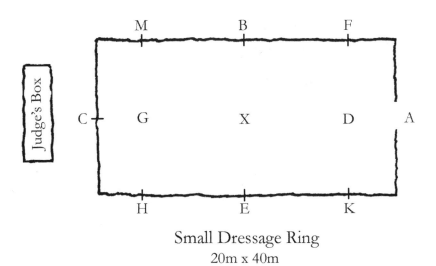

Small Dressage Ring
20m x 40m

The next week when I rode Duke into the arena for our lesson, Heather was pacing off distances around the perimeter. She positioned big plastic cones with large letters at different points around the ring. I had been studying the dressage pattern she had given me and began visualizing our route between the different letters. I had also bought a book on *Dressage for Beginners*. I had carefully studied the photos and suggestions. Until now, I had been a spectator, someone on the sidelines watching with objective interest, only an observer. All of a sudden dressage was no longer a spectator sport for me. Now there was the chance that I could be terribly humiliated or get seriously hurt, or both.

"Let's do our usual warm up before we run through the dressage test," suggested Heather, as she plunked down a cone with the letter "E" on it along the side of a ground pole marking the edge of the practice dressage ring. As I squeezed my calves to signal Duke into a trot to warm up, I tried to recall the first movement in the test. I couldn't remember. My head felt a little dizzy. I grabbed onto a hunk of Duke's mane to steady myself as we trotted around the ring.

Heather positioned herself just outside the perimeter of the ring she had marked off, reached into her pocket, and pulled out a piece of paper. "For now, I'll call out each movement to you. After a few times, I'm sure you won't need that," Heather informed me. "You'll have one minute after the bell to enter the ring and begin the test." Heather looked down at the paper. "At A, enter working trot," began Heather. "At X, halt, salute; proceed working trot." I urged Duke forward and looked straight at C, where the judge's box would be. "At C, track left; at E, circle left 20 meters." Heather's voice was loud and clear. As I listened for the next instruction from Heather, I relaxed my grip on Duke's mane and concentrated on feeling the rhythm of his trot. Maybe this would be fun after all.

I quickly found that I was good at memorizing the riding patterns. We never made a wrong turn or incorrect movement during these practice sessions, even after Heather stopped calling out what was coming. These mental and physical movements with the horse, flowing one into the next, reminded me of Tai Chi. The focus and attention to the movement I was doing and of what was next kept me from feeling self-conscious. As long as I could keep the concentration, I did not lose the momentum.

Entry forms for the next Dickson show were pinned up on the main barn door, with a large note from Heather: "To all students: Fill out and turn in to me by Friday." There really wasn't any choice here. I knew that I was being included and that it was part of the curriculum. As I left the barn that day, I took one of the forms to fill out.

For the next few weeks before the show, I could hear each movement being called out in my head whenever I was by myself. When I practiced with Duke, I would say the movements aloud to him as we went through each one. I hoped that if I forgot something, he would take over and do it correctly.

All of us, students and Heather, were ready to head over from Circle V Stables to Dickson Ranch early on the Saturday of the show. Heather would trailer two horses at a time over to Dickson and then return for the next two—in the order of the scheduled test times. Because Duke and I were at the lowest level, we were in the first horse trailer shuttle run. After we had loaded Duke and the second horse, I hopped into the cab of Heather's truck. "Don't worry about your warm up. There will be plenty of time for me to make a couple more trips to get horses here, and still put you through some exercises before your number is called," reassured Heather. I didn't know if I felt thrilled or scared. I looked out the truck window and silently recited the movements of my test as we drove the few miles down Sir Francis Drake Boulevard.

Once we had unloaded the horses from the trailer, I found a quiet, shady spot to tie Duke. I hung up a feeder filled with hay for him. He calmly began munching, while I went about getting saddle and bridle ready. Just as she had predicted, Heather appeared as I mounted Duke and walked him into the warm-up arena. It was about 20 minutes before my number would be called.

"Trot a 20-meter circle." "Bring him to a square halt." "No walking." "Half halt." "C-A-N-T-E-R." "Keep a steady rhythm; no rushing." Heather kept us moving during the warm-up. She glanced down at her watch and motioned me to the gate. "I know you've got butterflies. Keep them flying in formation," chuckled Heather.

As Duke and I approached the dressage arena, I could see the previous rider doing the ending salute to the judge. The judge's box faced into the arena at the far end of the ring, but allowed space for horse and rider to pass by on the outside of the dressage ring in front of the box. We would have a few minutes to warm up going around this track and in front of the judge's box. I nudged Duke into a trot around the outside of the edge of the dressage ring. I remembered that I needed to trot or canter him past the judge's box from both directions during the warm up around the ring. Duke should see the box before the test so that he wouldn't be startled by it when we were doing the test.

As I circled around in the other direction, the bell rang, letting us know that we had one minute to enter the ring and begin the test. We headed for the opening into the ring. A number of Heather's students called to me from the railing: "Good luck, Katherine," "Go for the blue." "Don't break a leg."

As we went across the diagonal of the ring halfway through the test, I began to relax. I was doing it! I felt as if I wouldn't fall off or do any worse than I had done so far. I found that I never enjoyed the nervous energy or anxiety in starting a test, but, after I got past that (halfway through), and could see that I could do it, I enjoyed it. I loved the feeling that I could do it, knew that I could do it. Going in, I never started out that way. It was only after I could see that I could do it, was doing it, that I truly enjoyed myself.

My canter depart had been on the correct lead. As I headed down the long side and into the last canter circle, my foot came out of the stirrup on the side away from the judge's view. If I could just pick up the stirrup again before we came out of the corner, nobody would notice, at least, maybe the judge wouldn't see that. I lifted my shoulders and wiggled my foot around trying to get it back into the stirrup. After a couple of tries, I got it. I shifted myself in the saddle to be more balanced as we trotted through the next corner and then down center line for our final salute. I leaned forward and patted Duke on the neck as we turned past the judge's box and rode out of the dressage ring.

Heather and her students greeted me with claps and cheers as we came through the gate. "Good job, Katherine," called Pam. "You did it," cheered Patrick. "Good show," congratulated Meadow. And then, "It was all very quiet except for the clanking of your stirrup," called Tony. Everybody laughed. I felt incredibly relieved that it was over, and forgot about the lost stirrup.

I took my time unsaddling Duke, brushing him down, and finding a comfortable, shady spot until it was time for us to trailer back to Circle V Stables. The dressage test results would not be posted for an hour or more, and I was certain that my name would be too far down on the list to get any mention. I went to the food booth, got an orange soda, and sat by the dressage arena to watch the rest of the rides in my division.

"Let's go over by the announcer's table," called Heather. "The Green Division scores have just been posted on the board." We all crowded around to catch a glimpse of the list of riders and their test scores. For my category, Green Division, Test Level I, fourteen names were listed in order by score, from highest to lowest. Brightly-colored ribbons, pinned with a name label, were lying on a table near by. Heather nudged me and exclaimed, "Look, Katherine. You got 5th place," On the table, I saw a beautiful, pink ribbon, with my name on it. I stood up straight and tall as I pressed forward to grab the award. I couldn't wait to show Duke and hang it on his stable door.

Story 10
Breathe into the Paper Bag

✦

(April 1987)

On Duke in the Cross-Country Phase at Dickson Horse Trials

After some years of boarding my Quarter horse, Duke, at Circle V Stables in Fairfax, we moved with Heather to Windfield Station in Nicasio. We were still close enough to compete in the horse trials at Dickson Ranch and had been riding in the Green Division for over a year. I was competing with Duke in the dressage and stadium jumping phases by this time.

But I was still on the sidelines watching Heather and Duke going cross-country. Dickson Ranch was a great place for beginning riders in all phases of horse trials—in dressage, cross-country jumping, and stadium jumping. Green riders could start competing with the basics—the simplest dressage test. Then they could enter the more difficult jumping phases when they felt ready for them. Confidence could be built and experience could be gained, one phase at a time. Individual riders could win ribbons in one phase, which encouraged them to try their best even if they were not eligible for overall ribbons.

Duke and I began with the dressage phase, with Heather competing with him in stadium jumping. This third phase of the trials at Dickson Ranch was ridden in an outdoor arena through a course of about ten to twelve jumps. Stadium jumping was scored by penalty points for jump pole knockdowns and for time through the course. It showed that the horse was still going well after the cross-country phase. Once Duke had learned the routine in the stadium jumping phase with Heather, and I felt confident enough to handle that, I rode both dressage and stadium jumping. Then we entered him in the cross-country with Heather. Duke was doing all three phases—with me up in dressage and stadium jumping and Heather out on the cross-country course.

The competitive spirit was not what spurred me on. Fear of failure and injury dampened that. I wanted to master the movements and ride the tests, but didn't feel any desire to beat somebody else. I felt exhilaration when I finished the dressage test without being eliminated for an incorrect movement, or when I came over the last jump in the stadium jumping phase still in the saddle.

When watching Duke and Heather out on the cross-country course, cantering along in the open field popping over the log jumps, my heart ached to be out there, feeling the movement, the breeze on my face, and grappling with how to approach the next obstacle. I longed for the excitement of following my riding strategy as we approached a jump, giving Duke the right cues, and then sailing over the obstacle in a steady, even rhythm.

The cross-country course, to me, was much different than the dressage and stadium phases. I lacked the confidence in my abilities because of my limited experience and few opportunities for success. Going cross-country, over logs and down drops that were fixed and solid and didn't just fall away when you bumped them, was much more frightening. If you came over one of those jumps wrong, you were in for much bigger consequences. It felt scary, but I thought about what I had done already. I recalled how the dressage test and the stadium jumping had also seemed scary.

Finally, I came to Heather: "I want to do the cross-country. Do you think I'm up to it?" "Sure. We'll start practicing next week," she replied.

The owners of Dickson Ranch allowed riders to come and practice on their cross-country course going over all the jumps for a small fee. This was another great service they provided to beginner riders. Typically, advance practice is not allowed in horse trials. I could never have learned something so frightening, without being able to take baby steps, one at a time.

The following Friday afternoon, we loaded Duke into Heather's old horse trailer and piled all his tack into the back of her truck. As we drove the 20-minute ride from Windfield Station to Dickson Ranch on the Nicasio Valley Road, my insides began to bounce in rhythm to the outsides of the truck and trailer. Heather pulled up next to the jumping arena. We lowered the ramp on the trailer. Duke backed out slowly.

No one was around the stables. We tied Duke to a railing and unloaded the equipment. "Let's do a little warm up in the jumping arena before we go out into the cross-country course," said Heather. I put my foot into the stirrup, grabbed a piece of Duke's mane, and launched myself into the saddle. Heather set up a jump with two poles up on standards at either end and crossed as an X in the middle. "Get Duke moving in a good balanced trot. Come straight to the jump. Keep the rhythm," called Heather. Duke was his usual steady and reliable horse self. He didn't hesitate or act concerned. Because of the training Heather had done with him and as was his nature, he knew what he was supposed to do and popped right over the X jump.

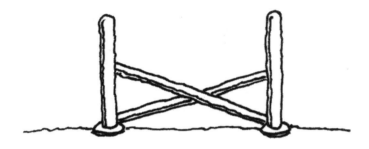

Heather shifted the poles at the jump, lifting up one end of a pole to make a cross bar to set up a 2-foot upright jump. We circled around, still at the trot, and popped over it. As usual, I was repeating my mantra in my head: "Eyes up, heels down. Look to where you're going."

"Okay. That's great. Let's go out into the first field." Heather walked alongside. We headed out of the arena and over to the path that led into the big open field with the cross-country obstacles. The cross-country jumps were made from cut tree trunks, laid across the track, and positioned solidly with stakes at either end. There were a couple of double combination jumps with smaller logs.

Duke pricked up his ears in anticipation as we came up into the field. It was the first time that I had been on a horse out in the cross-country field in the middle of all the jumps. A winding track circled the field with five or six jumping obstacles laid out along its path. I looked across at the first jump, a large tree trunk laid across the track. All of a sudden, I couldn't breathe. I opened my mouth wide, and tried expanding my lungs. No air came in. I choked a little. I tried again. It felt like someone had pulled a plastic bag over my head and was now tying a rope around my neck. I felt dizzy. I felt like I was suffocating. It seemed as though the sun was going down.

"Katherine, what's the matter? Your face has gone white," cried Heather, as she looked up at me. "I can't breathe," I gasped. Heather grabbed Duke's bridle and yelled: "Get off, and lie down on the ground. I've got hold of Duke. We'll be right back." As I got down on the hard, rocky ground, Heather hopped up on Duke and rode back to the barn at a fast trot. Minutes later she returned, jumped off, and handed me a paper bag. "Here, breathe into this. Slowly. You can do it."

After a few gulps and coughs, my breathing became steady and regular. "Guess you were hyperventilating. When you get back on, I'll have you ride around in the field for a while. Forget about any of the obstacles. Instead of going over any of the cross-country jumps today, we'll set up a couple of poles out in the middle of the field to trot over." As Heather dragged a pole onto the field, I signaled Duke into a trot. I sucked in a deep breath as we jogged along the track and maneuvered around the cross-country jumps.

Knowing that we wouldn't be jumping any logs today gave me back my confidence. I turned Duke toward the poles that Heather had set up in a small X jump. I knew I could do this. And I knew that after we were jumping over X's and uprights out in the field, I would be able to pop over a log. My fear subsided and exhilaration set in.

Story 11
The Humane Society Is Called

✦

(July 1987)

Jumping with Duke at Dickson Ranch

After moving her training operations from Circle V Stables in Fairfax to Windfield Station in Nicasio, Heather cut back on the number of students she taught. Duke and I were part of her contingent at Windfield Station. This beautiful and well-designed facility was one of the most elegant horse stables in Marin County at the time. The horsewoman who ran and owned Windfield Station was a gentle and kindly person who enjoyed the company of her horses more than the company of humans. She had a manager who took care of dealing with the barn business and the boarders, many of whom were quite demanding. I kept my distance from other boarders and their squabbles and politics. I just did my thing with Heather and her students.

The biggest challenge in my riding continued to be establishing myself as the senior partner in the horse-human relationship. I was hesitant to correct when necessary. I was also tentative and unsure when to reward. Duke, at times, took advantage of my lack of confidence and ignored my instructions. I clearly understood that such a partnership could be dangerous, to both Duke and to me. If my horse didn't respect or trust me and I was not able to call the shots, we were in for trouble. I did not want a 1200-pound animal I was sitting on to tell me what he would or would not do. For me to be confident and (relatively) safe, I had to be able to trust him to do what I asked. At this point, I was always wary of how Duke might behave.

Correction usually involves a nudge or kick in the ribs, a jerk on the reins, or a swat with a whip, without hesitation. Timing of reward and correction, for the horse to understand, is critical. For me, it just took a long time to realize that my little nudge in the ribs was easily ignored. So I was under-doing what was needed, or responding too late. Reward for the horse is making him as comfortable as possible, *not* causing him any discomfort. It is allowing the horse to be relaxed and easy, giving relief from any correction. A soft pat on the neck with "Good boy" or "Good girl" reinforces the reward. I knew that I needed to reward or correct at the exact moment or it was pointless.

I needed to learn to be in charge, to command respect from this herd animal who knows only too well how to push others around, whose nature is to try for top stallion or lead mare. I know being the senior partner minimizes the possibilities of the horse causing injury or death. In particular, mine. If the horse ignores what I ask, we could get into serious trouble, into dangerous situations. I had seen a number of incidents at Windfield Station, and at other barns, where riders were not the senior partners, but were subservient to their horses—a dangerous relationship. I completely understood why I needed to learn this. Learning this was not easy. Heather was quick to notice and repeatedly remind me not to back off and allow the horse to take charge. Duke was willing to do what was asked of him as long as the rider exuded confidence that she knew what she was doing and made it clear to him that he couldn't avoid or evade the task at hand. It took me a long time to establish this kind of relationship with Duke.

Heather began riding when she was five, at her own insistence. Growing up in a suburban area outside of Detroit, she let her mother know, through tantrums and coercion, that she had to become a horsewoman and a skilled equestrian. First, through training in the hunter-jumper discipline, and later in three-day eventing and dressage, Heather developed her skills to become an exceptional rider. Her intuition and communication with horses is uncanny, and she shines when she enters into competition.

In my training with Heather and my horses, when I listened, understood, and followed her instructions, I was successful in what I was attempting. There were times when I literally put my life in her hands (and survived). I saw some of her students ignore her suggestions or disagree with them. I always saw failure or mild disaster in those cases.

Duke and I had been working on our canter departs and had been getting the correct lead consistently for some time. We had made significant improvement. It was rare that I didn't get the correct lead. Duke knew the signals but could be stubborn at times and would be, on occasion, very resistant. After all, he was a horse, and that was his nature and his right. Duke's personality definitely had a stubborn streak.

On one particular day, maybe he had slept wrong or had a slight stiffness that had gone unnoticed. As we were going through our routine paces in our lesson at Windfield Station, Duke would not take the correct lead. It didn't matter whether it was his good side or bad side. Horses are better balanced going to one side or the other just as we humans are right-handed or left-handed. I gave him extra help by using the reins to keep his head to the inside and better balance him. But even with this added assistance, Duke just wouldn't take the correct lead when we went into the canter depart. It became a matter of doing it until he did it right, and not ending before that—not rewarding him when he wasn't doing the correct movement. With Heather's help, Duke and I had worked through problems many times. Key to this was not rewarding the horse by letting him get away with resistance and disobedience.

Usually our riding lessons in the arena took about 45 minutes. Sometimes we rode for an hour or so if there was some particular thing that needed more work to get it right. The arena lessons were always punctuated with walk breaks, so we could both catch our breath. I knew it was very important that we finish up doing whatever it was correctly, so that Duke would have come away with this in his mind. Duke knew how to get the correct lead. He had been doing it for Heather for years. He had been giving me the correct lead consistently for many months. What seemed to be coming up this day was his just deciding he didn't want to do it and his lack of respect for me. Heather could have gotten on and he would have been responding correctly in an instant. But that wouldn't teach me anything, and it didn't show Duke that I could do it.

"Show him the open door, Katherine. Once you get it, then you can reward him," said Heather. That open door to Duke was the reward for doing something correctly. For me to show it to him, I had to close all other avenues of response. I had to give him a correction if he had the wrong response, but make life extremely comfortable if he did the right movement. I must make it clear to him exactly what I wanted, show Duke how to follow my instructions. And when he did what was asked, comfort and praise were his rewards.

We would have to get the correct lead at least three times in a row, both sides, before Duke's reward would come, before he would be praised and go back to the paddock to munch hay. So we continued beyond the usual one-hour lesson. After going for about 15 minutes longer than usual, a woman came out from the barn. She walked into the arena, came up to Duke and me, and told me that I should stop immediately, that I was being cruel to the horse to ride so long. I didn't know who she was or why she was saying this to me. I felt bewildered and confused and could barely focus on what I was doing or should be doing.

Heather took it in her stride and just ignored the woman. I was concentrating hard on the riding task at hand and we had finally gotten the correct lead. This interruption was disturbing and distracting. "Please go away. We are working here," I mumbled, without looking at the woman. She went back into the barn.

Within the next few minutes, I got the three good departs in a row. "Good. Better. Better. You need to end on success with Duke. He will be ready and willing to give you this next time out," explained Heather. Duke had finally gone through the open door. Heather headed for home. I walked Duke around the arena to cool down. When I dismounted and took him into the barn, the same woman who had come out earlier came up to me and said, "You'll have to wait until the officer arrives. The Humane Society was called. They're sending an officer out."

How could anyone do this? My throat got dry. My heart started pounding. I stammered as I tried to say something in my defense. Tears welled up in my eyes. I realized that I would be thought guilty before being even considered innocent. Just being accused of mistreating an animal put me into the guilty category. Would I get arrested and be taken to jail? For what? What had I done? I hadn't used my whip. I wasn't wearing spurs.

To ride in an arena for an hour and 20 minutes? What the hell was that? Many horses are ridden out on rugged trails for hours, even for days.

I felt frightened but also very angry. I hollered at the top of my lungs: "Somebody here needs to get a job, a real job, in the real world." My voice echoed off the walls of the barn. This was the only thing I could come up with at that moment. I trudged off to unsaddle Duke and put him back in his paddock.

As I sat against the fence at Duke's paddock and waited for the authorities to come and bring me up on charges, I did the best I could to keep from crying and from imagining what disaster this would do to my life, to my riding career. A Humane Society truck drove into the ranch and up the lane to where I was sitting. A woman in a uniform with an official insignia hopped out and introduced herself. I looked her in the eyes, "I didn't do *anything*. I just rode my horse a little longer than usual in the arena, and somebody here reported it as a horrible crime." My voice quavered and tears rolled down my face. "Oh, we get this kind of thing all the time from these humane-iacs. Such busybodies. Sorry, but we are required to come check them out. I just need to verify that your horse is okay. No biggy," she pronounced.

The officer from the Humane Society walked over to Duke, who was quietly munching his hay in his paddock. As she came to the fence, he looked up. She opened the gate and walked over to him. Duke went back to his hay. She ran her hands along his neck, his back, and his sides, looking closely at his coat. "Not a mark," the officer pronounced. "Not even any sweat or dried sweat. Somebody's wasting my time." She came out of the paddock, walked back to her truck, got into the cab and slammed the door. As she drove past the barn, the officer gunned the engine a bit. Dirt sprayed up as the truck sped out the main gate and onto Nicasio Valley Road.

Story 12
Have Trailer, Will Travel

◆

(August 1987)

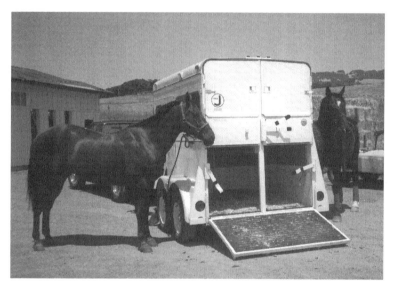

Duke (on the left) at Flying Cloud in Petaluma

At least once before each of the horse trials, we would trailer Duke with another horse and rider over to Dickson Ranch to practice. Linda, a woman about ten years younger than I, also one of Heather's students, was competing in all three phases and had her own truck and trailer. She and her horse had moved up from the Green Division into Novice Level and she was enthusiastic about winning. She regularly invited Duke and me to join her to drive over for a practice ride at Dickson. It was an opportunity for me to ride out in the cross-country course and just have some fun. Duke and I could trot and canter out in the field and get comfortable being on the course. No pressure to go over any of the jumps.

Linda would first practice diligently in the jumping arena, having her horse go over all of the jumps that were set up. Just before the return trip to Windfield Station, she would position her horse in the start box for the cross-country course, and then call me over. "Here's a stopwatch. Give me the signal and press that button." Linda handed down the stopwatch to me. As I dropped my arm to signal and pressed the button, off they would go onto the course. I enjoyed watching them take each obstacle at a good canter.

One evening before one of these arranged practice days, Linda phoned. "Katherine, I can't go tomorrow. Do you want to take the truck and trailer and go with Duke by yourself? Wait. On second thought, maybe you should go out and do some practice driving my truck and trailer. Then you'll be ready to borrow it whenever I can't make it. You can buy me a tank of gas. I'll leave the keys under the mat on the driver's side. Don't back into anything. And don't forget to get me the gas." She hung up the phone.

I had never driven a truck and horse trailer, but had certainly spent lots of time as a passenger in such a rig. On trips with Heather or Linda, I had helped out with loading and unloading the horses, which was usually uneventful, something I could handle. Duke was easy to load and trailer. He would just pop right into the trailer and wait for a wedge of hay. I had driven my brother's truck on occasion and knew how to handle that.

As a teenager I had been obsessive about learning to drive a car, and had gotten my learner's permit the day that I turned fifteen-and-a-half. Then I set about coercing my father to teach me to drive. For the following six months until I hit the legal age to take the driver's test, I would patiently wait every Saturday morning until my father had finished his breakfast and second cup of coffee. Then I would hover closer, until he would finally put down his newspaper and take me out in the family car for a driving lesson. As soon as we got to the frontage road near the old city dump, my father would stop the car and wave me into the driver's seat. I would shift into first gear and my coaching session would begin.

These images flashed through my mind as I dialed my brother Geoff's phone number. He drove a truck on a daily basis in his pool and spa business and often towed a trailer for special equipment. "Hi, Geoff. It's your sister. Remember how dad taught me to drive? Well, I need to drive a friend's truck and horse trailer, and better get some practice. Can you give me a driving lesson tomorrow? We'll leave the horse home for this first go." "Sure," he laughed. "Is this out at Windfield Station? And how is 'ole Duke these days? What time should I meet you?"

Out at the ranch the next morning, I hopped up into the cab of the truck and reached under the mat for the keys. Geoff started around to the passenger side, and then stopped and motioned to me. "Come out a minute, and let's check the hitch and ball," he advised. I remembered then how Heather and Linda, too, had always inspected the hitch carefully before driving off. Geoff put his foot up onto the hitch and ball and put his weight on it. "Always make sure this is connected properly." His advice was carefully noted.

As I started the engine, and we buckled our seat belts, my brother turned to me. "First thing we'll practice is backing up. Pull out on the dirt track, and then put it into reverse to back up and turn around." "Starting right off with the advance course, huh?" I chuckled. As I put the truck into reverse and turned the steering wheel, the truck moved in the direction I expected, but the trailer angled in the opposite direction. If I kept going, there would be a collision or a jackknife. Yikes. I was backing Linda's horse trailer into an oak tree.

"Hold it. If you want the trailer to go to the right, turn the steering wheel to the right, clockwise, just the opposite of the way you think it should go." Geoff laughed. "Pull forward and have another go." He shifted around to watch the trailer and the back of the truck.

I spent the next hour maneuvering the truck and trailer as Geoff directed on all the paved and dirt roads on the Windfield Station property. While the truck was in low gear, the left side of my brain was in high gear. How to turn the wheel to get where I wanted to go was counter-intuitive when I backed up. But as long as I took my time and thought about what I needed to do to get the truck and trailer to do what I wanted, we did okay.

"All in all, pretty good, big sister. I must say. If you need a job driving a truck, let me know. I have lots of connections." Geoff patted me on the back, unbuckled his seat belt, and hopped out of the truck cab. I now felt that I was ready for the public roadways.

There was a small gas station a couple of miles from the ranch with easy access from Sir Francis Drake Blvd. I would be able to drive in and through without backing up. I knew that the first thing Linda would do after walking around to check for any damage would be to check the gas gauge. As I pulled into the gas station, almost clipping the gas pumps, I felt great elation at my independence. This kind of freedom was what I needed for my riding adventures. But I wanted to be filling my own gas tank of my own truck, not somebody else's. I didn't want to be waiting around for an invite from someone else to go for a trail ride or trip to Dickson Ranch. I decided it would just be a matter of time, a fairly short time, before I had my own truck and trailer.

Story 13
We Ride Over the Speed Limit

◆

(September 1988)

Waiting to Go Into the Starting Box at Dickson Horse Trials

If anyone had told me during that first year of riding lessons that in less than five years I would be riding in a cross-country competition, I would not have believed a word of it. So when I write this story, I am amazed at reading my own words.

Heather stressed dressage as a discipline that would pay off in the jumping arena and on the cross-country course. Learning to ride dressage movements was the key to becoming the senior partner in the rider-horse relationship. It was quite clear to me early on how right Heather was. If your horse couldn't or wouldn't do what you were asking, there would be big trouble. The horse had to learn to trust me and not resist my instructions. I had to believe in and trust the horse, trust that the horse would do what I asked.

Along with training the horse to learn what was being asked, the rider had to be ready to demand obedience for movements the horse knew and was capable of. My lack of experience and confidence made this the ultimate challenge: to ask the horse for what I wanted, to reward him if I got it, and to instantly correct him if I didn't get what I asked.

This is what was going through my head on an early morning in the fall of 1988 as we loaded Duke into the trailer and headed over to Dickson Ranch to compete in a one-day 3-Phase Trial. It was two years earlier that Duke and I started to compete in the dressage test. Heather had ridden him in Phase 2, the Cross-Country, and Phase 3, Stadium Jumping. The second year, I began riding the stadium jumping phase. This year, the third year, I rode Duke in all three phases. With some tribulations and exhilarations along the way, of course.

The fear of failure I had first felt when I started riding lessons was now overshadowed by the fear of injury. I had actually come to a point where I looked forward to riding the dressage test. The chances of getting badly injured seemed much less than in cross-country or stadium jumping. My body tingled and my mind floated with happiness each time I completed a dressage test with some success. Just finishing the test, no matter how many mistakes I made, felt like success. Overcoming my nervousness and focusing on the horse and on the dressage movements was also charged with success for me.

This day the dressage went pretty well. It was the last of the 3-phase trials that Dickson Ranch would hold this year. When the scores came in from dressage, I was actually in 4th place. A white ribbon would be ours at the end of the day. I was excited and pleased. Heather signaled for me to come to one of the warm-up arenas to get ready for the cross-country course. She smiled: "You should have gotten 2nd or 3rd. You had those other riders beat." Such comments from Heather always made me feel good.

Heather set up some practice jumps. Duke and I went through our routine: a few times over an X jump, and then a few times over a 2-foot high cross bar. Then, over the loudspeaker, a voice boomed: "Number 43 in the start box; Number 44 up next." My number was 44. My mouth suddenly felt dry. As Duke and I walked to the starting box, the butterflies in my stomach began bumping into each other.

The cross-country course at Dickson Ranch is laid out on two large fields. The starting box is at the top edge of a dry creek bed. Each competitor rides down a track through the creek bed and then up out into the first field. As we waited briefly in the starting box for the time keeper to press the stop watch and give us the signal to go, I tightened my grip on my crop, pressed hard down into my heels, and grabbed a hunk of Duke's mane.

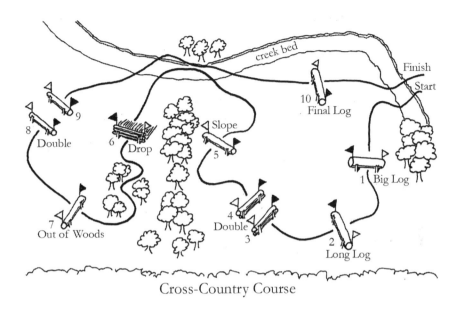

Cross-Country Course

The timekeeper looked up at us, dropped his arm to signal, and pressed the stopwatch. I nudged Duke with my heels. Off we trotted down the track into the dry creek bed and up the other side. As we came up out of the creek bed, Duke took one look at the open field and all the jumps, and decided he didn't want any of this today. He made an abrupt halt, and began to turn around to head back toward the starting box.

I didn't think; I couldn't think. The crop swatted Duke on the shoulder. It startled both of us. Duke straightened out and took off into the field at a fast canter. We headed directly toward the first jump. My intuition and right brain had taken over. "Heels down; eyes up; keep the butterflies in formation," I muttered to myself. It felt like we were cantering at 100 miles an hour. We took every jump, in the right order, and stayed on course. As we rounded the first field, I was still on Duke's back.

After jumping all of the obstacles in the first field, we shifted down from the canter and settled into a steady trot. I kept my eyes up and held on tightly to the crop as we trotted through a grove of oak trees and into the second field. My stomach no longer ached. I was conscious that I was still aboard. Duke was paying attention and doing everything he was being asked. He was into his usual matter-of-fact, workman-like manner. I signaled Duke back up into a canter, and we sailed comfortably over the jumps through the rest of the course.

When we rode back up through the dry creek bed and crossed the finish line, I felt that I had truly passed the test and with flying colors. Heather was off getting her next student warmed up. A couple of my friends who had come to cheer me on were still out on the course. We walked over to the stable area and I dismounted. Exhilaration and pride welled up inside me. I didn't need anyone there to congratulate me, tell me how I looked or how I did. I just felt great accomplishment. I was so relieved that this part of the day was over. It didn't matter how well I had done but just that I had done it. After that, I knew I would be capable of handling the stadium jumping later in the afternoon.

For the cross-country phase, horse and rider are tested for speed, endurance, and jumping ability. The jumps are solid and don't fall when bumped. Penalty points are given for such things as a refusal to jump an obstacle, omission of an obstacle, and exceeding (or coming in under) the time limit. If your horse cut out at a jump or jumped obstacles in the wrong order, you could be given penalty points or be eliminated from the competition. The cross-country times and penalty points for the green division were posted at the officials' table about an hour later. Duke and I had come in *under* the optimum time for my division. I could not believe my eyes when I looked at the score sheet. As I thought back to how fast it had seemed, I realized it was fast, very fast. We had exceeded the Green Division speed limit. In order to level the playing field and give chances to less-experienced riders, the Dickson Ranch competition rules penalized riders who came in faster than the time set for their division. This encouraged better riders to move up into a more advanced class. I was thrilled to get demerits for going too fast. In the cross-county green division, I had won the RED ribbon—second place!

The day became somewhat of a hazy blur. Now, I just wanted to finish the jumping phase and celebrate our great victory. But the day wasn't over yet.

Late in the afternoon, we suited up once more and warmed up for stadium jumping. Heather made certain Duke and I did the necessary practice. Knowing that she would put us through the proper paces was a great comfort.

"Number 44 up next," sang out the loudspeaker. The bell jingled. Duke and I entered the jumping arena and halted. I nodded my head and lowered my arm in a salute to the judge. Duke set off at an easy trot. We were in no rush at this point. As we approached each jump, I rattled off my checklist in my head: "Heels down," "Eyes up," "Keep a steady, even rhythm." Duke must have heard every word. He never missed a stride, and took each jump smoothly. As we rounded the final turn, made the last leap, and rode through the finish markers, I heard a few cheers and clapping. I leaned over and patted Duke, and praised him for being so good.

Now the sun was low and the show officials were off tallying the results. Heather and I and another student were sitting on a bench watching riders and horses prepare for departure. The loudspeaker in the jumping arena buzzed. The announcer began with the overall ratings, starting at 5th place and reading upward. Then we heard it: "First place overall, Katherine Maxwell riding Duke." Heather squealed, and I started to cry. A large blue ribbon was waiting for me at the announcer's table.

Story 14
Duke Takes His Final Jump

✦

(August 1990)

On Duke Jumping the Brick Wall at Windfield Station

The most painful part of the experience of losing a horse you own and care about is the nod to the veterinarian—the required agreement from you that this is what must be done. The next most difficult is knowing that this could happen again with another horse.

Duke and I had been riding partners for seven years. We had improved enough in our dressage and low-level jumping to move out of the Green Division and up into Novice Level at the Dickson Ranch Horse Trials. At this point, Duke had reached his athletic limits. He started cutting out just before jumps that were a bit higher than we had been doing. We had done okay that summer, finishing up our last horse trial with a couple of ribbons in that next division up of Novice Level—5th place in dressage and 3rd place in jumping.

In lessons, Heather had upped the top jump pole an inch or so. After this, more often than not, Duke would abruptly cut to the left just before the jump and avoid going over. I hardly ever stayed on, which was no fun. When Heather rode him, she would set him up to the jump more expertly and be able to get him over. After a couple of weeks of this, Heather said, "We don't want to insist on anything that is beyond his physical and athletic abilities. We need to bring him back to an easier and more comfortable level for a while, re-build his confidence."

We made a plan for the fall to ease up on jump height and do more gymnastic jumps. It was always fun and rewarding to practice over a gymnastic line: a carefully laid out row of jumps that taught the horse how to jump. In these gymnastic lines, three or four jumps were spaced close together, at the right distance for the horse's stride. The horse was encouraged to continue through and not cut out between jumps. We started having a good time again. I stopped worrying about getting dumped. As Duke built back his confidence, mine also returned. My balance improved to the point that I could keep my arms extended out to the sides and stay in jump position through an entire set of gymnastic jumps. It was thrilling. I could tell that Duke was having a good time, too. We were going back to basics and he was doing well.

With horses, as with other experiences in life, it's often when you least expect something bad, that it happens. Duke and I had gone through a lot together, learned a lot together. As he had become trained and competent in each skill under Heather's instruction and supervision, I then learned from him. I relied on him for kindness and patience, and had usually gotten that. When I didn't, I had been scared or angry or both. Duke and I had built a relationship—much trust, some distrust. He had learned to trust me not to ask for more than he was capable of, not to ask him to do something that we couldn't do. He had also learned how to take advantage of me. We had a long-term relationship.

One early afternoon in the late summer of 1990, I received a phone call from the owner of Windfield Station. "Duke has a bad injury to a back leg. He must have kicked the wall of his paddock shelter. His back leg is very swollen. He isn't putting any weight on it. You need to call your vet." I hung up the phone. A horrible feeling of impending doom rolled over me, as I dialed the vet's number. I prayed she could get out to the ranch with a moment's notice. I was well aware that, first and foremost, emergency treatment for a horse involved getting a message to your vet out on the road.

In the past, a few minor requests for the vet to come out to see Duke had been necessary, along with regularly scheduled checkups for routine shots and worming procedures. In these cases, I knew that it would be quite unusual for the vet to get there at the estimated time. Emergencies would take priority. Getting to and from ranches scattered around the county would add to the time. I had always been at the barn in advance of all vet visits, and came prepared to sit around and wait patiently until the vet arrived.

As I spoke with the vet's answering service, I tried to lower and steady my voice, to calm myself. "Yes, this is an emergency. My horse is out in Nicasio at Windfield Station. How soon can the doctor get there?" Everything seemed to be moving in slow motion.

"Keep to the speed limit," I said to myself as I headed out the back road to Nicasio. "Driving too fast could get you a ticket, or cause an accident, and make it worse." I knew that I would get there first, and the vet wouldn't be there for a while. Nothing could be diagnosed or done until then. I parked my car close to the barn and sprinted down the row of paddocks to where Duke would be. He stood awkwardly with his head hanging down. He had his weight shifted to one side, with the near back leg barely resting on the ground. The lower part of the leg was horribly swollen. Duke just stood there. He didn't turn his head toward me as I came into his paddock.

For the next hour, I talked to Duke softy and brushed his coat. He shifted his weight a bit, but hardly moved from this position. I felt very lonely. From that moment, I missed him, knowing that our time together was possibly over.

The vet arrived and immediately administered some painkillers. X-rays were taken, and a careful and thorough examination by touch was done. "I can't be certain until we get the X-rays developed, but it looks and feels like he has multiple fractures in his lower leg. From the look of the swelling, there may be some damage to his hock, the joint in the hind leg that corresponds to the knee. If that's the case, it's doubtful that he could walk without extreme pain, even with some success in surgery," the doctor explained. "The painkillers will make him more comfortable for now. It will take a couple of hours for me to get back to the lab at the office, get the x-rays developed, and see exactly what's happened. I'll call you."

As I walked out of the barn with tears streaming down my face, some boarder said to me: "Gee, I don't know who to feel more sorry for, you or Duke." I bit my tongue and hurried to my car. A few hours after I returned home, the phone rang. It was the vet. "I'm sorry, Katherine. It's about as bad as it could be. There are multiple fractures in that hind leg and the hock is shattered. There have been some successes with surgery for fractures, but absolutely nothing can be done for the hock. I can be out there first thing tomorrow morning with the handler and take care of everything."

It took me a couple of weeks before I could go out and clean out my locker at the ranch. When I did go, I went out late at night. I knew I couldn't take talking casually to anyone out there, at least not for a while. A month or so later, Heather and I had our own special ceremony to commemorate Duke, reminisce on his virtues, and on his bit of stubbornness. He was an old friend who would be missed for a long time to come.

Story 15
An Arab Gets Adopted

✦

(January 1995)

Heather on Dal Royale, nicknamed Abou, at Dougherty Ranch

After Duke's fatal accident, I rode an English Thoroughbred for a time. This demanded some attention and kept me from being too sad about Duke. Heather and I had done a couple of years training and riding with this horse when he began pulling up lame in his back leg for months at a time. The vet could not determine what caused the trouble or actually what it was. So he retired to a small ranch in Northern California.

I was a rider without a ride. And I showed little enthusiasm for looking for another horse. "Maybe we can find a horse that needs to be apprenticed for exercise or needs a home, one we can adopt," Heather suggested. "This could be a good way to get us going again." It was early spring. After the frustration of not riding much that winter, the suggestion appealed to me. Off we went to ask around and check out tack shop bulletin boards.

A few days later Heather called, "I just talked to the gal at Marin Tack and Feed. We may have a possible ride. There's a young college student with an Arabian gelding she's had since she was a kid. Now she has no time for him because of class work. She just wants to find him a good home, someone who will make sure he gets cared for and exercised. I think we should go take a look." "Sounds okay to me," I replied with a little trepidation. "Just let me know where and when for the test drive."

I had heard lots of horror stories about how hotheaded Arabs were, but it still sounded wonderful to think about riding again. I knew that Heather wouldn't put me into anything over my head, or more dangerous than I could handle. She always seemed to know just how much adrenaline was healthy and not harmful and how far I could go without courting disaster. At least, I hoped so.

One late afternoon the following week, Heather and I drove over to an unincorporated area beyond San Anselmo. At the address we were given was a small pasture enclosed with barbed-wire fencing. A red-coated, rather plump Arab gelding dozed on the hillside. He opened one eye to look at us as we walked up. He was very fuzzy with a heavy winter coat from living out in the open.

As we were looking him over, a Honda Accord pulled up and a cheerful woman in her early 20's hopped out. "I see you've met my boy, Dal. That's short for Dal Royale, his registered name. He's more interested in visitors when they bring carrots. My family and I have always spoiled him. I've got a saddle and a bridle in the trunk, if you want to try him out.

There's an open field just down that track." Heather nodded enthusiastically, as we followed the Arab's owner to her car.

We tacked up the chubby Arab and escorted him down to the field. His owner chatted on. "He's about 23 years old now, maybe older. I've had him more than ten years. Great on the trails, but he doesn't like to ride in an arena, gets upset, especially when there are jumps about. A couple of times I tried riding in an arena with jumps and Dal spooked so much I had to get off." I glanced over at Heather, and could see that glint in her eye that said: "Well, he's not going to get away with that. He's not going to tell us what to do. *We'll* be the senior partners."

Heather swung herself into the saddle. "I'll just take him for a quick ride and see how he is." Off she went. As Heather started out, the little Arab's tail began to swish and his ears went back, in a displeased manner. As he trotted off with his tail swishing and his ears flattened, I suspected that he might be calculating how he could dislodge this rider from his back.

The owner chatted on to me, about Dal's likes and dislikes, and what a great family member he was. As she talked to me, paying no attention to Heather and Dal, I kept an eye on how the ride was going. I looked past the owner and could see that my suspicions were correct about Dal and that he was not interested in going for a ride, or having anyone on his back. He had other ideas, probably wanted to return to dozing in his pasture. Dal wasn't bucking or spinning, but looked like he definitely was thinking about such evasive tactics.

The little Arab pinned back his ears and swished his tail harder. Heather didn't have a whip. She took hold of the reins close to the bit and gave a hard, downward jerk. Her heels dug into his sides for a quick moment. The horse made a little hopping step forward, and set off at a nice brisk trot. His ears went forward and his tail relaxed. There would be no more questioning of what he would be doing on this ride. Dal had quickly realized that this rider wasn't going to put up with any shenanigans. Heather now had his attention and his respect. I hoped that I could do the same.

After circling the field a number of times at walk, trot, and canter, and in both directions, they headed back our way. "He's got a balanced trot, lots of energy. I'm sure Katherine will take great care of him. We'll certainly get him into better shape." I knew that Heather also meant: shaped up. Heather was never on that endless quest for the perfect horse. She was on the lookout for what the problems were, to determine if they were challenges she would enjoy or were just too much trouble. I studied Heather's face and could see right away that she was already thinking about the exercises we would be doing to get this little Arab on track and what a thrill it would be.

We all agreed that this could be a good match, and would talk later in the week after we had all had a chance to think about the arrangements. After the Arab's owner had driven off and Heather and I were in my car, I said to her: "Should we get a vet check? Isn't that always standard routine for a new horse owner?" Heather looked at me with a twinkle in her eye: "Haven't you ever heard the expression: 'Never look a gift horse in the mouth?'" Ahh. Now I truly knew the meaning of that saying.

Story 16
The Complaint Department is Closed

✦

(August 1996)

Trotting Abou, aka Dal, around the Outdoor Arena at Dougherty Ranch

If you avoid dealing with an issue with a horse, the problem keeps coming up and usually gets worse until you may be faced with a life-or-death situation. I learned that I must expect the best behavior from the horse, but must be prepared for the worst, must be ready for it. I constantly reminded myself (or Heather did) that I had to give the horse the chance to do it right, not anticipate what he might do wrong and hang on him or prematurely give a correction.

In the earlier years of my riding, particularly with Duke, I would pray the horse would respond properly to my aids and not object, not force me to insist on his behaving. I found out that avoiding giving the horse a correction when it was needed just didn't work. At some point, the horse will question you, challenge you, will be the herd animal that he is. If the rider doesn't stand up to this challenge, the horse will typically take greater advantage and try to make the rider the junior partner in this horse-human relationship.

Soon after I had adopted Dal Royale, the feisty little Arab, we gave him the nickname, Abou, a name quite suitable to his nature. He was like the monkey in *One Thousand and One Arabian Nights*—reddish-brown and mischievous. In my five years riding Abou, he taught me how to take command and become the senior partner. If you were a skilled and competent rider who could immediately establish who was the senior partner in the horse-human relationship, you could ride Abou with no trouble. Other than Heather, I haven't seen many riders who can do this. Abou certainly knew he had met his senior partner when Heather was on his back. I was another matter—or, I should say, partner. If you were not able to tell Abou, in no uncertain terms, that he was going to mind his manners and do what you signaled, you were in for trouble. "Abou was your greatest teacher," Heather would remark years later.

Shortly after I adopted Abou, we moved him to the Dougherty Arabian Ranch in Nicasio. It was much closer to home, and it seemed that a ranch with Arabian in its name suited Abou. It was the summer of 1996.

Under Heather's guidance and reinforcement, I had convinced myself and Abou that we could ride in an arena with jumps set up. This was no longer a problem, or so I thought. His previous owner had lamented that she was unable to do this, and, on a couple of occasions when she had taken him into such an arena, Abou had spooked, shied, and bucked. He refused to follow her commands. She had immediately dismounted and taken him back to his pasture, where he could lounge and graze. Abou had learned what he could get away with and had this firmly implanted in his intuitive memory.

For me, there was a specific moment in time, of enlightenment, with Abou. It was like those jokes I have heard about that sudden awakening. We came to the edge of a cliff, and I clearly understood all of a sudden what was needed to survive, what I must do to avoid getting seriously injured.

I had made major strides with Abou performing dressage movements and getting him to respond to my instructions. But there were those days when he just didn't want to work, was just not willing to be the junior partner. On those days, Abou had many ways to evade doing what you asked of him. He had even bucked me off on a number of occasions. Abou wasn't about to do what you wanted if you weren't ready to truly, and instantly, let him know he had no choice. For years before we met him, Abou had scared the hell out of more than one rider by shying, spooking, jumping to the side, spinning around, rearing, and bucking. The only thing that he ever allowed without any protest was a nice, slow trail ride. That was what he enjoyed.

Heather had clearly let him know that she wouldn't put up with that kind of misbehavior. She wasn't going to put herself or the horse in any kind of danger, and Abou knew it. He was always pretty much a perfect angel when Heather was on his back. If, for a moment, he forgot who she was, she reminded him quickly. For me, this was not the case. Abou didn't pull his stunts every time we rode. So he could easily lull me into thinking he was over such arguments.

Then a day would come when he just wouldn't have any of it. Abou would try spooking at something he had seen a thousand times. If I didn't take him to task and correct him with a tap on his rump, within a short time, he might rear or buck me off. Heather would make sure I corrected him and then get on with the work. On those occasions when I got dumped, I always got right back on. I had to get back on or he would certainly get worse. In fact, by the time I hit the dirt, I felt angry enough and resolved enough, though delayed, to get Abou on track.

So this one morning, we were working in the large outdoor arena at Dougherty Ranch. I knew right away that Abou was feeling cranky. He kept putting his ears back and swishing his tail every time I gave the aid (leg and seat signal) to trot or canter. "Keep your whip ready. If he doesn't respond when you use your leg, don't kick harder. Give him a tap with the whip. He knows what he's supposed to do. He's just being disobedient. Don't ask him. Tell him. Tell him that the Complaint Department is closed," Heather instructed.

But this time I didn't give a correction as Heather instructed, immediately and without hesitation. I just tried kicking a bit harder. I didn't want Abou to buck me off and dump me in the dirt. I was reluctant to have an argument with him. We were cantering near the edge of the arena, when, all of a sudden, I felt a sharp, grating pain and a hard, rough scrapping along my outside leg. Abou was purposely running me into the fence. He was trying to scrape me off. Abou thought he had found a new way to avoid paying attention, a new evasion for his special bag of tricks.

Panic welled up inside. My stomach got queasy. My face felt hot from the anger that he was deliberately doing this to me. This time I knew without a doubt that he wasn't surprised or frightened. Whenever Abou spooked or shied, I always wondered briefly if maybe there really was something that was scaring him. There was no question here. There was nothing scaring him. He was deliberately trying to harm me, and being incredibly disobedient. This Arab was being very bad and very dangerous. I reached back with the whip and gave him a whack on his butt, as Heather's words exploded in my head: "Don't ask him. Tell him. Tell him that the Complaint Department is closed." I would probably get dumped either way, but I knew that I had better do something. There was a much better chance of surviving without injury if I corrected him instantly rather than letting him get away with misbehaving so badly.

As the whip stung Abou's rear end, he made a short, energetic hop. He quickly moved away from the fence and settled into a rhythmic canter back on the track he was supposed to be on. Suddenly, Abou became a model citizen—nose down, even rhythm, no resistance. "Good for you, Katherine. Just what that little stinker needed." Heather was right on, as usual. Abou never put me in the dirt again. He rarely ever argued with me after that day. I became the senior partner.

Story 17
The Dream Horse is A Mare

✦

(February 2000)

With Isabella, aka Vanity Santana, at Dougherty Ranch

The arrival of the year 2000 brought a different transition for me than most of those celebrating the New Year. As the clocks rolled over with everyone watching their computers for signs of a Y2K meltdown, I was about to hit 60. Amazing, incredible, fantastic. But I was again a horseless rider. In May, while grazing in pasture, Abou, my little Arab, had been kicked so badly by another horse that he could not go on. His loss was a tragedy that I had not yet sorted out. During these six months after the accident, I caught a ride here and there with no clear direction and very little enthusiasm. I wondered if my time on the back of a horse was up for good. To hang up my spurs, as they say, seemed to be the logical thing to do. But I just couldn't look into the future without a few more rides.

If I could just have one more second chance—that's what kept running through my head. Then one day, I asked myself: Why couldn't I give it another go, find another horse? And, what exactly was it that I wanted from this one last chance? I knew a lot more at this point than I did the other times I had looked for a horse—about myself, about horses, and about what I wanted from both. This time I didn't want to start from scratch with a totally green horse. I didn't want to invest a lot of time training before really riding. I would rather set aside a bigger budget (within limits) to find a horse that had some good, basic training. I wanted a horse that had some mileage, was athletic, and still young enough to learn along with me.

After 20 years, I began another list, much different than the earlier one, a list of what I wanted in this horse, from this ride. In my mind, the first two considerations were breed and gender. The next were age and then price. I reviewed what I knew firsthand, what I had personally seen secondhand, and what I had read about third hand. Under breed, I listed: Quarter Horse (a breed I had already had a good experience with), Hanoverian (a warmblood with a good reputation), and Irish Thoroughbred (with a question mark next to this one). As to gender, I wrote: gelding. Certainly, a stallion was too much for me as such energy was for most riders, and mares had bad reputations for being cranky and irritable. There were always one or two stories circulating in the barns about some sorry owner who had to deal with a problem mare. I didn't even consider "mare" as an item to put on my list.

As to age, that fell into a range of from 5 to 9 years old. A horse any younger might not be physically mature and would not have had enough time for some good training. Any older, he might be a bit too set in his ways, physically and mentally. The last item on my list was how much was I willing to spend. For this, I took into account that I would not be going for any high-level competitions and so would not need a horse with expensive lineage and coveted heritage. I determined I would look for a healthy gelding, of a youthful age, with a good attitude and some basic training. These criteria would put the price in a comfortable range for me.

"Heather, can you meet me for lunch? I have given it some thought and decided what I want to do next in my riding. I want you to help me find a horse." "That sounds like fun," exclaimed Heather. "When do we start looking?" I chuckled: "As soon as you look over my list of priorities."

A few days later, I passed my list across the table to Heather as we sat down in a local café. She studied each item, and nodded her head. "Excellent. Excellent. We can start by checking the bulletin boards in the tack shops. Can you buzz up to Offutt's Tack Store in Petaluma and get a copy of Ride Magazine? They have a good Horses for Sale section." We were off and running. Or should I say cantering? After my months of low spirits from being without a ride, now we were both headed out to see what we could find in the horse trader market.

During those next six weeks, we came across several horses that seemed good possibilities. We would make arrangements with an owner or trainer and drive out to some barn to take a test ride. There was an 8-year-old Morgan gelding in Woodside that we thought was too expensive for his physical capabilities. Then, a 6-year-old Hanoverian east of Santa Rosa, whose gaits were uneven and awkward.

Then one day, Heather called: "I know you didn't have 'mare' on your list, but this trainer I know from the Lodi area has an ad for a 4-year-old American Saddlebred. We hadn't thought of this breed either, but they are lovely. They are called pleasure horses. And, yes, I know she's a year younger than you noted. But we haven't had anything to look at lately. Should I give her a call and get more details?" "Oh, sure. Why not? Since there's nothing else right now, and I need a ride," I replied. I went to the bookshelf with all my horse books, and found an encyclopedia of horse breeds. The photos of this Kentucky-bred horse looked wonderful. The descriptions included rave reviews: comfortable, well-mannered, durable, exhibits great brilliance, proud head carriage. But a mare? And a 4-year-old was rather young.

Heather called back the next day. "Can you take Tuesday or Wednesday off, so we can drive out near Lodi in the Sacramento Valley and check out this mare? The trainer has been working with her on dressage for about six months. Apparently, she is smart and has a lovely temperament. The owner that this trainer works for breeds Friesians. But this Saddlebred mare got into the mix somewhere, and they don't want to keep her. The asking price is quite reasonable, definitely within the budget you set." "All right. Let's go. Hopefully, it won't be raining," I commented.

That next Tuesday, the sun was shining as Heather and I headed east on Highway 80. We followed the trainer's directions and had no trouble finding her small barn. Five black Friesians grazed in the pasture. We were shown through the barn and introduced to each of the other horses in their stalls. The trainer then opened the last stall, grabbing a halter as she entered. "This is Vanity Santana, granddaughter of Sultan Santana, a talented harness racer in Kentucky," she proclaimed as she led out a black Saddlebred mare, with four white socks and a small white blaze on her forehead. "I'll go get a saddle that you can use. You can ride her out in that fenced pasture." She pointed off to the east. Heather smiled and reached for the lead rope. Once the mare was saddled and bridled, we led her out to the pasture.

Heather hopped up into the saddle, still smiling. Off they went, briefly at a walk, then into a trot. "Oh, this is heaven. What a trot. So smooth. Not like anything I have ever felt. I've heard about these Saddlebreds. Pleasure horses, that will calmly jog the plantation all day. Smooth. Smooth. Smooth. Katherine, you have got to get up on her." But Heather didn't stop or slow down. She moved the mare into a wider circle and had her go up into a canter. It was beautiful, so beautiful. The dark, elegant head and neck bobbed gracefully. The long, sleek legs seemed to prance and flow in a perfect 3-beat rhythm.

It took Heather a long time to finish riding. She just didn't seem to want to get off. Finally, she headed over to me and dismounted. "You are not going to believe this, Katherine." I scrunched up all my courage and walked over to take the reins. I held the reins, grabbed some mane, and put my foot into the stirrup. Then I was on Vanity Santana. "Trot, Katherine. Trot. You won't believe it."

I gently squeezed my legs against the mare's sides, signaling her into a trot. Something was happening. It didn't feel anything like any trot I had ever ridden. No bouncing. I could sit this trot with no trouble. I knew that "Saddlebred" should go on my list. And I should definitely not rule out a mare.

Two weeks later we were back in Lodi. We had arranged to have the mare trailered over to a reputable vet's office in the area to get a vet check. If everything was thumbs up, Vanity Santana, the 4-year-old American Saddlebred mare would be coming home with us. While we waited, the vet administered the routine tests. Heather was almost hopping up and down. I looked at her sternly. "Don't get excited until after all the results are in. We have to have a healthy horse."

The vet came out from the small, adjacent barn, and motioned to us: "This mare is in terrific health and great condition. Go into the office. I'll give you some paperwork for verification." As we loaded the mare into the trailer, I joined in with Heather's enthusiasm. I could hardly contain my excitement. What kind of new adventure would this be?

Story 18
Do It Until You Own It

✦

(February 2005)

Isabella on the Lunge Line at Dougherty Ranch

"Do it until you own it." That's what Heather was always saying to me. What that meant to me is move the knowledge from the left side of my brain to the intuitive right side, get my body to memorize it, not just my mind. I have been able to do this. My regrets are few with my riding efforts—even though I am not a natural athlete and I have been slow in building my confidence. The ride has been bumpy, but it has also been delicious. Now more than ever, I continue to savor the moments.

Isabella is the nickname we gave to Vanity Santana, the American Saddle-bred mare. She has been my riding partner for more than five years. From the moment we met, her good nature and intelligence made it a joy to get into the saddle. Not that she hasn't tried to take charge or have her say or given some resistance here and there. But as a horse, and smarter than most, Isabella has needed few corrections, and has been very willing to do what is asked of her.

We have worked on dressage movements and taken a go at some low-level jumping. Heather had gotten out of the horse training and teaching business years ago, but she continued to give lessons to Isabella and me on an irregular basis. We have made steady, quiet improvements in our riding—nothing earth shattering, all very pleasant. I had no particular goals or focus until two things happened that were significant in my riding.

This is exactly how the first dramatic thing happened. It was on Tuesday, February 9th, 2005 (not just any Tuesday), somewhere between 1:30 pm and 2:00 pm. For some months previous, we had been focusing on such dressage movements as leg yielding, half passes, and extended trot. As was our usual routine, we started this lesson with Isabella and me doing warm-up exercises. We then went into a serpentine pattern across the arena, first at the walk and then at the trot. Somewhere in the middle of that hour, my balance in the saddle shifted, became more centered. My riding position suddenly changed—absolutely for the better. I could feel this amazing alteration, subtle yet incredibly significant. My balance was on center, more on center than it ever had been. When I dismounted, I didn't say anything to Heather about this. I wondered if she had noticed or if it was all my imagination.

When I went out to practice on my own two days later, I was curious to see if I would experience this same significant shift in how I could ride. I got on Isabella and we started our usual routine. I was astounded. Yes, it *was* different. I felt so balanced and centered. When Isabella went up into the trot, it was like never before. What was happening here? Was I finally *owning it*? Had I finally done it enough to own it? It felt so great. I would have to come back again in a few days to see if it was still there. And I wanted to find out if Heather had noticed this subtle, but amazing, change.

But the next week, Heather didn't make it to the barn. It was two weeks before I saw her. She had moved to the San Jose area, and it was much more difficult for her to get to Marin on a regular basis. During those two weeks, every time that I rode, it was the same. Amazing! I decided, that rather than concern myself as to whether the new balance had taken, I should just forget about it, sit back and truly enjoy the ride.

The minute Heather showed up at the barn two weeks later, I blurted out: "Heather, something's different, very different. It's fantastic. My center of balance seems to have shifted." I described to her what had been going on since last we met. "Well, let's get going and see what's happening," she urged.

We tacked up Isabella and led her into the indoor arena. I mounted and started our warm up. "Wow, you're right. It is different! So much better. Your center of balance has shifted. Ever so slightly, but so much better. Let's go through some trot and canter movements," Heather offered. The breakthrough didn't fade.

The second significant thing was six months later. Heather moved much farther south and would no longer be able to ride with us. She had given me more than I had imagined, had opened doors for me and shown me a world I never knew existed. How lucky I have been to have had such a teacher and a friend. After almost 24 years, we hugged goodbye. I would miss her for the rest of my life.

The all-girls team that had been three members was now only two. I would have to rely more on myself, and Isabella would be more dependent upon me. This would certainly make a shift in our relationship. It was after months of aimless fooling around that I looked Isabella in the eye one day and said: "We need to do something. We need to plot a new course, set some goals. We need a coach." Isabella looked back at me, but didn't say anything. I imagined she preferred taking it easy, that she was content to just graze in pasture.

Now I was no longer interested in the thrill (and fear) that came with jumping. My practice and work in dressage had, up until now, been a means to an end. The dressage movements that I had mastered were fairly basic. I knew that there was a broad scope of what could be learned, and I determined that dressage training with a good teacher would be the best path to follow for Isabella and me.

How would I go about finding an instructor—someone that I could respect both as a rider and a teacher? I didn't want to move to another barn. I didn't want to join another class of school-age children. I didn't have a dressage saddle, and worried about the time and effort it would take to get used to one. Would I be able to find a teacher who could be patient with how long this might take me?

One morning at the barn, I was chatting with one of the owners of Dougherty Ranch, Diana. I told her of my interest in dressage and my concerns. "Katherine, the trainer who had been boarding Sugar, my favorite horse, rides dressage. I know she teaches and has an excellent reputation. Would you like me to give her a call?" I perked up. "Sounds good to me. That is, if she doesn't mind coming out here. I don't have a truck and horse trailer any more, you know," I replied. I had sold them a year after I lost Duke and had stopped competing. "And I need to make this as painless as possible. Literally, now that I think of it. Have you ever ridden in a dressage saddle? Have you ever felt knee blocks pressing on your calves? You really have to stretch down with your legs. I hope I can do it."

Two weeks later, I was sitting deep in a borrowed dressage saddle with my stirrup leathers longer than they had ever been, and Isabella was chewing on her new bit. "Use your upper leg on the downward transitions, and your lower leg on the upward transitions," Jeannette suggested. Isabella's left ear shifted back toward me, as she felt my signals and went up into a trot.

Jeannette is a talented and experienced rider and is proving to be a patient and skilled teacher with both Isabella and me. During our first two months of weekly lessons, all of the movements we were asked to do were familiar to both Isabella and me. Under Jeannette's coaching, I began doing leg yielding and shoulder in better than I had ever done.

But something I had not mastered, had not been able to do successfully, was walk-to-canter. Isabella knew how to do it with Heather on her back, but I had had lots of trouble and we had set it aside. As we came around a turn at the walk, I stretched down into the dressage saddle and pressed my inside leg against Isabella's side to keep her from cutting the corner. Jeannette suddenly called, "Canter." I didn't think about it. I just did it. I just gave the signal and we got it! Walk-to-canter—what a thrilling feeling. Could it get any better than this?

Epilogue

✦

(September 2005)

Riding Isabella at Dougherty Ranch

Over the last 25 years, I have had some amazing adventures with horses and horseback riding. I had learned so much from my horses and a good trainer, and they had learned from me. Memories of what happened to me began coming to mind when I started drawing and painting a few years ago at age 62. I thought back to 1981 when, at age 40, I took horseback riding lessons, knowing almost nothing about horses or riding and never having been particularly athletic. I knew from these earlier experiences that developing one's innate abilities is much more difficult as an older adult.

In recalling how I had learned new intuitive skills, I hoped to gain insight into applying the lessons I had learned and smoothing my path. So I jotted down these stories, tales of what had happened to me—how I felt, and how I ultimately handled a difficulty, or didn't. Then I could read my own stories and possibly apply their lessons to help me develop my art. I could use myself as my own learning model.

After graduating from college with a Bachelor's degree in Fine Art, I did little with my artwork. My artistic abilities and style went undeveloped and I did not pursue my art. Even if I had talent, I needed to earn a living. I got my teaching credentials and taught in public schools for a few years. From there, I took technical training to work with computers and found employment in the business world. It was about this same time that I made my list and began taking horseback riding lessons.

When I quit my corporate job in 2002 to become the technical associate in my husband's photography newsletter business, I soon realized that spending most days at a computer keyboard and solving website problems were not going to satisfy my heart and soul. As a treat to myself, I attended a drawing class at the American Academy of Equine Art in Lexington, Kentucky. This adventure greatly appealed to me because Lexington was the heart of the Bluegrass Country and horse heaven.

In the equine art class in Kentucky, I focused on having a good time, learning how to draw horses, and taking in the sights. I tackled the assignments and tried the best I could. To my amazement and enjoyment, I discovered that I could do the drawings fairly well. If I ever wanted to explore my artistic self, this seemed like the right time. Probably most of the brain cells carrying my artistic knowledge had been replaced by now. And any natural talent I might have had could have atrophied. But I wanted to pick up where I left off after college and find out what kind of an artist I was, explore my innate ability.

In starting down this path—learning intuitive skills and resurrecting dormant talents—I felt I needed a plan. I wanted a practical course of action for guidance, encouragement, and insight, a way to develop any innate abilities and open me up to a creative place. I thought a learning model could help me—with ideas for how to get started, suggestions of exercises to practice, and a search for the best coaching. I didn't know what my artistic approach was or might be, but I wanted to find out.

I thought back to more than twenty years earlier at age 40 when I had started to learn to horseback ride, and not without difficulty. Through persistence, practice, and attention to the guidance of a good teacher, I had become a competent equestrian. I felt I could learn from my own stories of the many adventures I'd had. As I hit snags in my efforts to draw and paint, I recalled similar or analogous incidents that had happened with learning to horseback ride. I began writing down these stories of my own challenges, triumphs, and disappointments. In reading them, perhaps I could apply the lessons to my new adventure in art and gain strength and insight into these new challenges.

As my stories filled the pages, I thought that others might also be interested in reading them. I could not be the only one who has taken up something new to learn at an older age. As we live longer and enjoy better health, we have more opportunities to learn new things, whether it be computer skills, a foreign language, or an unfamiliar sport. So I offer you these stories that I wrote for myself to read when I get discouraged or when I need to remember what is important—of how I learned to horseback ride starting at age 40.

Glossary

On Duke in the Cross-Country at Dickson

Across the diagonal

After the rider and horse go along the short side of the arena, they turn towards the center of the rectangle and ride diagonally across the arena to the opposite corner. They have then changed the direction in which they were riding.

Aids

The aids are what the rider uses to communicate with the horse. The rider's body, seat, legs, hands and voice are considered "natural aids." The "artificial aids" are whip, spurs, side reins, martingales. The communication between rider and horse is by touch—that is, with the horse's reaction to the rider's seat, legs and hands.

A leg up	A leg up is an assist to help a rider get into the saddle. Someone holds the rider's bent left leg and boosts her or him up into the saddle. For me, a mounting block works best to get into the saddle.
American Saddlebred	Isabella is an American Saddlebred. This breed was developed in Kentucky by plantation owners in the early nineteenth century to provide a good-looking animal who gave an exceptionally comfortable ride. This was essential for long hours spent in the saddle. This all-round pleasure horse could then be hitched to a carriage to take the family to town on the weekend. The Saddlebred is valued for its good disposition and great stamina. From my own experience with Isabella, this description is quite accurate.
Appaloosa	Heather's school horse, Aggie, was an Appie. The breed is descendant from Spanish stock brought here by the Conquistadors. The Appaloosa is noted for its spotted color, which was prized and developed by the Nez Perce Indians who lived in Palouse country, of the Northwestern states. The Appaloosa has a short, strong back, powerful hindquarters, with good, hard feet.
Arabian	My horse, Dal Royale, nicknamed Abou, was an Arabian. The Arab is the oldest of all horse breeds and adapted to life of a harsh environment. Because of their stamina, these horses are particularly suited to the sport of endurance riding. The short, refined head with dished profile and graceful curving neck are this breed's most distinctive features.
Breeches	These riding pants are made of a stretchy material and have flat seams, so as not to chafe against the rider's skin. They go to the ankle and fit inside knee-high riding boots.
Bridle	The bridle is a horse head harness that has a crown-piece, cheek pieces, noseband, browband, bit and reins.

Canter	A three-beat gait where horse's legs on opposite sides lead and strike the ground at the same time. This gait is faster than the trot and slower than the gallop.
Chestnut	This horse coat color ranges from dark reddish brown to light golden brown.
Cross-country	The second phase of trials is timed and ridden at speed over natural fixed jumps.
Dressage	From the French word for training, this discipline teaches the rider and horse how to do various gaits and movements, with consideration of the natural physical abilities of the horse.
Dressage saddle	This type of saddle is designed specifically for dressage riders. The rider is positioned in the center of the saddle and with a long leg, through a deep seat and knee blocks.
Farrier	This term refers to a person who shoes horses and trims horses' hooves.
Field boots	These knee-high boots are similar to dress boots but have laces above the instep.
Friesian	This compactly-built horse was originally bred in Northern Holland and used as a war horse and as a mount for the nobility. The coloring is black with no white markings. Isabella's first training was with Friesians on a ranch near Lodi, California.
Gait	Gait describes the pattern of footfalls and the different speeds at which a horse can travel. Every horse has four natural gaits—(1) walk; (2) trot; (3) canter; (4) gallop.
Gallop	This four-beat gait is faster than the canter.
Gelding	A gelding is a castrated male horse.
Girth	Girth is the circumference of a horse's body, from behind the withers around the barrel. This also is the name for the strap that holds down the saddle.

Green	A horse (or rider) that has just started training or is young and inexperienced is labeled green. This also refers to the lowest division in horse trials.
Gymnastics	Jumps are laid out in a direct line, are set specific distances apart, and are ridden through one after the other. This helps teach the horse how to jump and builds confidence for horse and rider at jumping heights and distances.
Hand	Hand is the unit of measurement used to estimate a horse's height and is supposedly the width of a man's hand, about 4 inches. Horses are measured from the top of the withers to the ground. The height of a horse is listed in the number of hands, followed by a decimal point, then followed by the number of additional inches. If a horse is sixteen-and-a-half hands, this is written as 16.2.
Hock	The hock is the joint in the back legs of a horse that corresponds to the knee joint in the front legs. It allows forward bending of the lower hind legs.
Lunging	To work a horse in a circle on the end of a long line or rope is called lunging. Voice commands are used to tell the horse what gait to take. Lunging is a way of exercising a horse and of reinforcing training by working from the ground.
Mare	Mare is a mature female horse, four years or older.
Mounting block	The portable stair step to assist the rider in getting up into the saddle is referred to as a mounting block.
Near side	The left side of the horse and the side from which riders usually mount the horse.
On the bit	A horse is considered on the bit when he carries himself easily, with good balance and impulsion, and accepts contact with the bit.
Phases of Horse Trials	The three phases in horse trials are (1) Dressage, (2) Cross-Country, and (3) Stadium Jumping, in that order.

Posting or rising trot	The rider rises up out of the saddle with each trot stride. When riding in posting (rising) trot in a circle, the rider needs to rise on the correct diagonal—that is, should be rising out of the saddle as the horse's outside shoulder goes forward. The horse is able to better balance himself if the rider is in the saddle when the horse's inside hind leg and outside foreleg are touching the ground.
Quarter Horse	The Quarter Horse is an American breed built and bred to run short distances at speed, originally a quarter mile.
Riding boots	Riding boots are knee-high boots that are designed to protect the rider's legs and feet from injury.
Sitting trot	The rider sits deep in the saddle without extending her legs as in a posting trot and does not rise out of the saddle.
Snaffle bit	This is one of the oldest and simplest bit designs and consists of a two-part mouthpiece with rings on the ends that attach to the reins. The action is on the corners of the lips.
Stadium jumping	This third phase of horse trials is an equestrian competition in which horse and rider ride a course of fences that are jumped in a specific order. Scoring is based on accuracy (e.g., penalty points for poles knocked down) and speed (time through course).
Stallion	A stallion is a mature male horse, that has not been castrated, usually used for breeding.
Tack	This is the general term for all handling, riding, and driving equipment used on a horse, as bridle, saddle, halter.
Tacking up	To tack up is to prepare the horse for riding by putting on saddle and bridle and any other equipment.
Three-day event	This competition is a combined set of test phases ridden over three consecutive days, which include a dressage test, a cross-country course, and stadium jumping.

Transition	A transition is a change of pace or direction—for example, from walk to trot, trot to canter, or canter back to trot.
Trot	This two-beat gait is when the outside hind and inside foreleg move forward together, then the inside hind and outside foreleg move forward as a pair.
Upright	This straight or upright jump has one or more horizontal poles set into side braces (standards) at varying heights.
Walk	The walk is a four-beat gait, with the sequence of: near hind, near fore, off hind, off fore.
Withers	The slight ridge in the horse's backbone, just behind the mane are the withers. This is the highest point on the horse's spine and the point from which height is measured.
X jump	This jump has two poles raised on the outside at the side braces (standards) that come together to form an X in the center, over which the horse jumps.

With Heather at Dickson Ranch in Fall 1987

978-0-595-38007-7
0-595-38007-7